R•A•V•E•N
TELLS STORIES

RAVEN TELLS STORIES

An Anthology of Alaskan Native Writing

EDITED BY JOSEPH BRUCHAC

The Greenfield Review Press
P.O. Box 308 Two Middle Grove Road
Greenfield Center, N.Y. 12833

Publication of this anthology has been made possible, in part, through Literary Publishing Grants from the Literature Program of New York State Council on the Arts and from the Literature Program of the National Endowment for the Arts.

ISBN 0-912678-80-1

Library of Congress #90-85173

FIRST EDITION

Composition by Sans Serif, 2378 East Stadium Blvd., Ann Arbor, MI 48104
Printed in the United States of America.

Cover art by Nathan Jackson
Cover photograph by Jean Flanagan-Carlo

CONTENTS

Martha B. Malavansky

Renee Matthew

Yvonne Mozée

Agpik-Robert Mulluk, Jr.

Frederick Paul

Jim Schoppert

Glen Simpson

Introduction

This major new collection of 23 Native writers, *Raven Tells Stories*, reveals the blossoming of the talent and energy of Alaska Native writers in the late 1980s and serves as a milestone in the development of contemporary Alaska Native Literature. In these pages, established voices join with newer ones to forge a bridge between two generations of Native writers. Alaska Natives have been conquering Western literary forms for at least a century, but this anthology reveals the depth, the quality, and the variety of that accomplishment today. Today, educators and the general public have expressed a strong desire to identify and collect the literary accomplishments of Alaska Natives; we hope that this anthology will help give Native writers the wider recognition they deserve.

The writers in this anthology come from the many distinct Native cultures of Alaska. Their traditional languages and life styles vary as much as does Alaska itself. Yet these writers are producing a literature which responds to the land and the changes in human habitation, and their insight into the Alaskan experience forges a common bond capable of binding the separate villages and the separate generations.

The older generation of writers in this anthology has lived through a period of rapid cultural change as village life was transformed under the influence of schools, modern transportation, and cash economy. Traditional languages, traditional economies, and cultural ways experienced enormous pressure. Often these writers warn of the problems inherent in rapid cultural change as well as describe those changes. They see Native values as capable of adaptive renewal as long as self-determination and basic cultural respect can be extracted from the dominant culture.

The younger generation is, in most cases, the first to grow up as true members of both cultures. In their explorations of identity and culture, they draw on childhood visions of a world already in flux, and seek to define themselves in relation to this moving and dynamic process.

Both generations of writers set their courses by a few fixed points along the journey. First, the land remains. Though there has been much destruction, Alaska's vast and varied expanse still reveals its wonder and power as it did to the Ancient Traveller from the Distant Time who is so popular in stories all over the North.

The traditional arts of song and storytelling were always important paths for personal expression, social instruction, and cultural definition, and they continue to provide inspiration for contemporary directions in written literature. These writers strive to create a written art which complements and reinforces traditional oral arts. The crucial source for this appreciation of oral tradition continues to be Native elders. Whether drawing from grandparents, uncles and aunts, or village elders, Alaska Native writers perceive the elders as those whose experiences are vital to any understanding of culture in a period of uncertain change. Their words, actions, and faces are to be found everywhere in this collection: the presence of Renee Matthew Singh's grandmother is felt though she is gone, and the elder who sits beneath the beaded cross in Josephine Fields' poem recreates the past through memory.

Lastly, the patterns of interaction with primal forces and observant animals continue to guide human understanding and appreciation of life in Alaska. Their attention to the animals of the distant mythic time and those that exist in the wild today assure that these writers will retain a wisdom and a way of moving through an increasingly technological world with respect and a sense of belonging as Roy Henry succinctly concludes, "Yes, I know those grounds." As the writers in this anthology use their experiences in this multi-cultural world, they reveal the vast importance placed on culture and tradition. However, they see culture not as a boundary line, or a treasure to be horded away, forever static and lifeless, but as a network of transactions and relations actively engaging values through change. Josephine Fields' poem of her mother doing beadwork to "hill billy" music on the radio, or Mary Lockwood's story about ice skates and a village boy show an acute awareness of the cultural transactions and negotiations which comprise contemporary Native experience. In much of the work here, change and continuity exist in an exchange which produces a constantly elaborating way of life to which the general term culture is often given. Of this experience, Robert Mulluk, Jr. writes, "Education we learned but we are still Inupiaq. / We act, think different but color and skin still Inupiaq."

These writers are aware of losses that have occurred. The pain of devastation and destruction of the land, of lifeways, and of some aspects of culture is severe, but for them, history is not oppressive. The past is not a burden, but a source of great strength and renewal. The people and the land are still here, and they speak clearly of the past. The future still seems capable of being molded by Native hands. The overpowering sense of pride these writers feel illustrates how history can liberate the present, free the imagination and intellect to destroy boundaries and limits. With a great sense of purpose, Edgar Jackson concludes:

I can look back
not in anger   or hate
but with respect for my people
myself
for believing in our traditions
accepting the changes
as the world passes into confusion
as we pass in silence towards freedom —

the freedom of choice.

Moreover, the work of these writers is charged with a mythic vision which helps establish connections between the present world and the older world with its creative forces. For Robert Davis, these connections are forged in a world between two darknesses and for Fred Bigjim they can be revealed when one's vision can perceive how "Spirit Moves" all around one in "primal creeping, misty stillness." For most of these writers, there is a spiritual power manifested in the sacred processes that they see around them. As the older village women say in a poem by Mary TallMountain, "Lots of spirits all over, this year." Raven still watches over his people; the Northern Lights still speak freely. However, to see these connections, to forge these bonds connecting humans to nature and spirit requires a quiet concentration, an almost meditative ability to look closely at the world around. Some of this intense, detailed observation can be seen in the poem of Nora Dauenhauer about Skunk cabbage, or Andy Hope's poem about dog salmon where (as Simon Ortiz has noted about oral literature) expression and perception become one.

Much of the writing in *Raven Tells Stories* is very personal, yet there are also pieces that hinge on political insights, and there is an underlying sense of responsibility that supports both orientations. The responsibility can be personal, familial, social, environmental, or cultural, but these writers sense the importance of their voices and thus the need to say something that will help, improve, and instruct themselves and others. Benson, Bigjim, and Simpson have written about injustice and alcohol-related problems. McGlashan and Fosdick have written about personal insights close to their lives. But their words all express an awareness of an accountability to others and to the world around them.

Perhaps the most essential goal for which these writers strive is to find in their writing and lives a sense of wholeness and balance. Rapid cultural change, various definitions of identity, and the competing perceptions of the future call for each writer to develop a personal vision of life in Alaska. Though they struggle to clarify a usable past, their eyes are on the horizon, their voices full of anticipation. In his poem "Between the Rock and the Walrus", Jim Schoppert expresses the tenuousness and unease of some of contemporary Alaska Native experience:

Ice beneath my feet
a crushing emptiness above
I stand between
the rock and the Walrus pondering
the conflagration of bridges
left behind. Before me lies
a web of lines criss-crossed
on a mirror.

James Ruppert
University of Alaska-Fairbanks

Diane E. Benson

I write about pain and recovery, I suppose, more than anything. I want to move people, cause them to experience sadness and then hope. Sometimes to laugh in the midst of despair. No matter what, hope is the outcome. I borrow from my life when I write more than anything.

Briefly, I have written all my life. Well, since I could first hold a pencil and make letters. Growing up in numerous foster homes and such situations breeding abuse, I escaped into writing. I was never the greatest at grammar, curiously enough, but I would say I have always been aware of the rhythms of speech. Although today I am an actress, I was very shy as a child. So, instead of talking, I listened to how other people spoke, made gestures, related to one another. In school, high school and college, it was rare, if ever, that I received less than A for any writing projects or essays. I say what I need to say, even tho my punctuation is always being corrected!

In 1985 I created Alaska's first contemporary theatre and performance group. The group was called Kokeena Improv, though we never did actual on-the-spot improvisations. I created scenes then worked on them with the five other actors. The pieces we performed addressed issues on land claims, corporate identity and its damage to tribal identity, alcohol abuse and death, and comedic situations about money versus tribal involvement. Our performances at the United Tribes of Alaska Conference in October 1985 brought the predominantly Native audience to their feet.

I have focused a great deal lately on my performing career. Presently I am doing a small role in the Disney film "White Fang," which will be released in 1991. Even though I am busy with such, I intend to write and continue writing. I want to be both an actor and a writer. I have no desire at present to give up either, and I know I will never quit writing unless my hand falls off! At which point I would probably find other means.

Sister Warrior

SISTER WARRIOR *is a One-Act play cen-*
tered in Southeast Alaska. The two main characters are
Billy, who is Native Alaskan, and Dora, who is white.
Angry and resentful after her friend has been killed, and
sitting in jail for robbing a liquor store, Billy responds to
no one until she meets Dora. "Sister Warrior" is about
two incarcerated young women who are friendless and
separated more by prejudice and their own ignorance of
each other's cultures. The play touches on differences,
but also on two different people's similarities as human
beings. Other characters include the matron of the jail,
Mrs. Reed, who serves as the villain, Tom Knight, a
police officer who tries to help Billy but doesn't always
do too well, Pastor White, a well-meaning missionary,
and Chicky, who faithfully brings Billy the news about
the outside world.

The play opened on March 5, 1987, produced by the
Theatre Guild, at the Red Ram in Anchorage, Alaska.

from SISTER WARRIOR, *a play*

BILLY

Get oughta here. (HE EXITS. SHE STANDS FOR A
SECOND THEN RUNS TO THE DOOR, TO SPEAK,
BUT HE CAN'T HEAR HER). I'm sorry about your
friend. (SHE TURNS AND TOUCHES *AMERICA* ON
THE WALL THEN TURNS AROUND WITH AN
IMAGINARY GUITAR AND STARTS SINGING TO
THE "ANIMALS" SONG:)

We gotta get outa this place! If it's the last thing we
ever doo . . .! "I" gotta get outa this place . . . finda a

better life for me and you . . .! Da . . . dum! Da . . . dum!
. . .

BROTHER WHITE

Hello there. (STANDING AT THE CELL DOOR, HE ENTERS ON THE SOUND OF THE ELECTRONIC RELEASE). How are you?

BILLY

(EMBARRASSED, BLURTS) When am I getting out of here?

BROTHER WHITE

I have no idea. Your foster parents haven't been by?

BILLY

I haven't heard a word from anybody. Besides, I hate that family.

BROTHER WHITE

I'm sorry to hear that. (PAUSE) I hear you have a cell mate. Dora? Where is she?

BILLY

She's taking her shower. What are you here for?

BROTHER WHITE

I thought I'd check up on you. I never really got to speak to you after your grandma died. I'm sure that was hard on you. (WAITS FOR A RESPONSE AND GETS NONE). I had hoped you'd be by the church. We miss you in the congregation.

BILLY

I haven't been there in a year.

BROTHER WHITE

And why is that Billy?

4

BILLY

I only went because grandma liked me to go.

BROTHER WHITE

We pray for you.

BILLY

Good. (SHE HAS PLACED HER BEADS ON HER LAP).

BROTHER WHITE

What do you have there Billy, you making something?

BILLY

No.

BROTHER WHITE

Are those the beads Fred gave to you?

BILLY

If you knew that then what the hell did you ask me for?

BROTHER WHITE

Mrs. Reed told me about the little incident that took place when you arrived.

BILLY

And I'm sure that they'll tell you anything else you want to know, so why don't you just go.

BROTHER WHITE

I came by because I was concerned about you . . . and I know you've had a hard time with the Harris family.

BILLY

What do you know? I had to live with those people treating me like a dog.

BROTHER WHITE

It couldn't have been that bad . . .

BILLY

Right. You know what? I ran away from home there once because they were drunk. They would drag me out of bed to watch them dance, and always making me clean their house right after school, while their own kids went out. When I ran away that time, I was gone for three days and they never even missed me. I went back because I was cold and hungry, but they never even knew I was gone.

BROTHER WHITE

I imagine that was painful; no one ever noticing you were gone.

BILLY

It doesn't matter.

BROTHER WHITE

The congregation is growing. (CAUTIOUSLY) We have a nice new family at the church. They love kids. I could use my influence with the welfare office . . . the family has expressed an interest in a foster child and I . . .

BILLY

I don't want to live with anyone! I don't need anybody.

BROTHER WHITE

Perhaps we can talk about that some other time.

BILLY

Whatever. Hey. Have you heard anything about a girl named Jo Jo? Do you know her?

BROTHER WHITE

Why yes, I do. As a matter of fact I saw her at the

hospital a couple days ago. Her hand was broken. It seems she went through a window or door or something. I didn't know you two were friends.

BILLY

What happened to her? How'd she hurt her hand?

BROTHER WHITE

I'm not sure. They say she smelled of alcohol when she was brought in. We were there singing hymns. There was a wonderful testimony from a young brother up there. One of the Joseph boys; maybe you know him? Very moving. The lord is coming soon Billy and we have to be ready. I can feel it.

BILLY

That's great. So, is Jo Jo still there or what?

BROTHER WHITE

I really don't know. I think she was being released from the hospital. Do you remember John 3:16? For God so loved the world . . .

BILLY

That he gave his only begotten son so that whosoever believeth in him shall not perish but have everlasting life. So?

BROTHER WHITE

So, I think you should think about it. At least you still remember the scripture. You were one of our best when you were little. You knew all the verses. We were proud. We have another Native girl there now who picks it up quickly . . . She even thinks of becoming a missionary.

BILLY

What for?

BROTHER WHITE

You used to think like that.

BILLY

Before I realized what a lie everything is.

BROTHER WHITE

I think we should pray. I have to be getting back soon.

BILLY

Don't let me stop you.

BROTHER WHITE

(PAUSE) I promised your grandmother when she was dying that I would do what I could for you, to pray for you, and to pick you up for church. I really don't want to break that promise.

BILLY

(MORE TO HERSELF) I don't want to break my promise either. (TURNS TO HIM). In the church, we're not suppose to wear jewelry, is that right?

BROTHER WHITE

That's right.

BILLY

That means I can't wear this necklace if I fixed it, could I?

BROTHER WHITE

We take our guidance from the scripture. It says in first Timothy that we are not to adorn ourselves.

BILLY

And, we can't eat fish eggs or seal grease can we?

BROTHER WHITE

It's not that exactly, it's just that there are scriptures . . .

BILLY

What scriptures? Does it say, "thou shall not eat fish eggs?"

BROTHER WHITE

Don't mock the Bible. There are things that are non-Christian; heathen practices and such that . . .

BILLY

Heathen!? Heathen!! Ha! "Why do the heathen rage?" Psalm 2:1. I remember you always used to use that word in church. I never knew it meant us!

BROTHER WHITE

Billy, you've really twisted . . .

BILLY

Okay Indians, repent! Being Indian is evil!! Isn't it Brother White? That's why missionaries go out into the world. To make people just like them. You. You came up here to Alaska, to do what? Save us heathens?

BROTHER WHITE

To spread the word! That is what God has put me on this earth to do!

BILLY

Well then, God wasn't thinkin' was he?

BROTHER WHITE

(CALLS OUT) Matron! Mrs. Reed! (ANGERED, HE PREPARES TO EXIT, THEN TURNS TO BILLY) I promised your grandmother. (MRS. REED UNLOCKS THE DOOR AND HE EXITS).

"Hostage of the Past"

Mother,
Grandmother watching
Mother, twisting, spitting, shaking,
Oily, slimy
suffocating the beaches of her soiled belly,
blowing
angry
Spruce screaming shame
shattered.
Grandmother watching
Boxed lives, tight ropes in between
travelling to desperation
connecting fragile beings
in motion too fast for hearing.
And if I dye,
my hair blue, what does it matter to you
words drip from lips with no sound anyhow.
Like those before me,
with less nobility
I peeled pride from your face
reaching through the bars
to touch the ancient
part of you.
Grandmother . . .
Watching, you
said it never happens to
our family.
But we *are* free, aren't we?
Police escort to Indian school
And it was true for you too
with missionary hand
that took your name.

And it happens,
I stood behind the bars of defiant submission
with self-indulgent stains on my face
Silenced like my sisters
mouths taped shut by raping power
Like my brothers
arm locked by poverty.
Locked behind bars,
Bars,
Bars where I wandered looking for the light.
Lights, neon, bright!
Right. Right.
Not Right.
The cells slams shut. Silenced.

It happens to our family,
man and woman kind
behind bars of mindless guidance
and historical mishaps of
economic barons.
Inmates of the U.S. Treasury
Yen King.
Locked behind the dollar,
behind bars of half truths
at the Inn of No Happiness.
And grandmother, quiet
watching with last breath
two days before Christmas.
She dreamed of peace
and fell anyway.
What happens to our family?
Family of man
Memory commemorations
Ceremony for the past
It has been 107 years
Since the U.S. Navy
Bombed Angoon
to support a trader

unwilling to pay
restitution for the
death of a shaman —
harpooned.
Children fell victim.
Grandmother, watching
Children fall victim
Are you watching?
Hollow eyes, deny
Mass graves in South Africa,
mass graves in Europe,
in Ethiopia, in Nicaragua, in Sitka!
Mass lies, mass hate,
Mass high,
At mass Noriega hides,
Mass numbers, mass serial, mass suicide,
Too high for the pain,
Genocidal recovery.
Family, like Panama, torn, drunk,
worn, turned out,
turned in, turned around.
Grandmother watching . . .
Raven
Call in the night.
Her spirit dances to volcanic reactions
Sounds of long ago —
The spirits before her
move the 7th Generation
Don't take oppression
The spruce stands tall
cedar fall with medicine
evoking the truth of our
indigenous ancestors
Our mother earth ravaged
We hang on —
Not gone.
Hostage of the 80's from Iran to Panama
I bought that too

as a hostage of the past
The notion we had vanished
at last.
Indigenous strong
Even with the slaughter of the Amazon.
Sparkles of past knowledge cling
to the trunks of our being
as long as one person stands
with Grandmother watching.

Fred Bigjim

Fred Bigjim, an Inupiat Eskimo raised in Sinrock and Nome, Alaska, holds two graduate degrees from Harvard University and attended law school. He is the author of *Sinrock*, *We Talk: You Yawn*, and *Walk the Wind*, and coauthored *Letters to Howard: An Interpretation of the Alaska Native Land Claims*. He has had poetry published in *We Make A Fire*, *The Alaska Quarterly Review*, and *The Wicazo Sa Review*. Soon to be published is *ANCSA*, a textbook on the Alaska Native Land Claims.

Developing Alaskan Native
Humanistic Themes

The Humanities discipline provides Alaska
Natives a natural and effective means for cultural
expression. As this discipline covers all the fields of
study that reflect our humanity, our emotional relation-
ships to one another, and the struggle to communicate
our feelings and dreams, it gives us the opportunity to
emphasize those things that separate us from other
peoples and cultures, while also finding common ground
with all other humanity. Art, architecture, music, literature, history, and philosophy belong to all cultures,
including Alaska Native societies. Through these, we
express what makes us who we are, and how we have
come to view the world and our place in it. The Humanities, then, offers a way to understand Alaska Natives
and maintain many of the traditional cultural values,
even in different immediate surroundings or in a foreign
environment away from the influences of our own culture. The Humanities also gives us an understanding of
the cultural values and life-view of those apart from our
own group and traditions.

As we look at ways to approach the study of the
Humanities, especially as they apply to Alaska Native
students, I would like to share some thoughts and
possibilities.

The interdisciplinary approach to the Humanities is
especially important. To fully understand ourselves and
our cultural heritage, we must have a knowledge of the
interdependence of forms of expression. Art is subject to
myth and philosophy. Music and literature are likewise
tied to philosophy and artistic expression. Native dance
is an art, a musical form, a telling of cultural history, a
statement of the philosophy of a people. To fully appreciate a sculpture or or painting, we must be able to relate
to the philosophical and historical background of the

work and to the mind of the artist. Literature, too, is an art form based within the philosophical foundations of the culture.

It is not difficult to identify Native themes in the Humanities that can inspire cultural expression in the literary, visual, and performing arts. We can explore traditional Native ways, i.e.: what the hunt meant to an individual and to the community; or what the legends and myths mean. We must develop a philosophical approach in discussing Native cultural expression, and we need to encourage the discussion of Native philosophies. There are a number of Native themes in the humanities that can be identified:

 — the themes that reappear in traditional stories (the role of man in nature, the supernatural universe, the social responsibility of each member of the community to others, etc.);

 — related themes that appear in traditional and contemporary arts (illustrations of myths and legends, themes of contemporary Native life);

 — traditional dance forms and musical styles and their related literary functions;

 — the role of religion and the spiritual world in Alaska Native philosophy (both before and after the introduction of Christianity).

We can provide an academic program which encourages Native student creative thought and expression on tradition, change, and identity by supplement programs as Tuma Theatre, Festival of Native Arts, and those using Native elders in seminars with more "academic" courses, such as Alaska Native Literature, (Alaska Native Poetry, Alaska Native Storytelling, Alaska Native Writings). The latter emphasizes individual creative accomplishments, while the former centers on group expression. Individual creative Native thought needs to be recognized, analyzed, discussed and shared in classroom settings. Through this type of discussion, there can emerge creative thought by Native students with the expression of tradition, change and identity.

The development of *courses* which would inspire

Native and non-Native exchanges of views would be helpful in allowing students to express the "authenticity" and "legitimacy" of Native cultures. This could be coupled with a greater emphasis on the "authenticity and legitimacy" of *all* cultures as they relate to the humanities. In one sense, this would join Native humanities with those of other groups, but in another sense, would validate them as equal to those that are traditionally identified in the field (such as the Ancient cultures of Egypt, Mesopotamia, and South America, the Classic cultures of Greece and Rome, the Moorish and Renaissance cultures, and the various periods of Modern humanitarian studies). This approach also allows for the constrictions of the University environment.

It is also important that some group within the university, perhaps the Alaska Native Studies program, assume the roles as advocate for young Native artists and writers. If these young people can be assisted in presenting their works before the public – something which I know from personal experience can be formidable and frustrating at best – they might find increased chances of success by obtaining this important opportunity to communicate with the non-Native population, establish a more sound basis for understanding between the two groups, and gain self-confidence and encouragement required to continue to express the deep and sometimes painful emotions involved in creativity.

We must also recognize the important variations within Alaska Native cultures. For instance, contemporary Native thought and writing is a broad topic. There are many different aspects to the Alaska Native community; Tlingit thought is not the same as Eskimo thought in many respects. Alaska Native studies could be incorporated as a major field of humanitarian studies with equal force to established traditional topics, such as "The Renaissance." As a part of the program, each Alaska Native group can be recognized for the individuality and special contributions of each. Themes for theater productions and dance ensembles, as well as for artistic and literary expression, should naturally emerge.

An in-depth look at Alaska Native people and their contribution to Native and non-Native history is also an important component of the Humanities. Again, there should be distinctions among different Native groups, emphasizing the contributions of each, and their individual histories. It is also important to include something of the Native "view" of history, the role of history and how it may differ from the traditional non-Native view of history and its role in development of cultural values.

The development of a course of study in the Humanities with special regard to the roles of Alaska Native groups can give us hope for the future of Alaska Native cultures and for a better understanding of them by non-Natives.

— March 1989

Spirit Moves

Sometimes I feel you around me,
Primal creeping, misty stillness.
Watching, waiting, dancing.
You scare me.

When I sleep, you visit me
In my dreams,
Wanting me to stay forever.
We laugh and float neatly about.

I saw you once, I think,
At Egavik.
The Eskimos called you a shaman.
I know better, I know you're
Spirit Moves.

Bowhead

Silently, I move toward destiny.
Quietly, you, Inupiat, await my destiny.

I can hear you as I move under the ice.
I can see you as I surface.

Together we wait.
Both know what the other thinks.

Although we live in different worlds,
We exist for each other.

I move toward you, Inupiat,
Because it is my destiny.

You wait for me,
Because I am your destiny.

Quietly, I approach you.
Silently you move toward me.

I give you your culture.
I give you myself, Bowhead Whale.

Reindeer

Antlers lowered.
Eyes glaring.
Hooves pawing.
Nose snorting.
Reindeer facing Inupiat.

Eskimo man cautiously continuing culture.
A rawhide noose ready to catch
A lifestyle.

The noose is thrown.
The struggle for life and culture begins.
Eyes of fear and panic,
Eyes of determination and survival,
Peer into each other.

It's over.
Inupiat begins the life process.
Reindeer provides the taste of life.
The Eskimo covers himself with the reindeer.
He continues his culture,
At least
For now.

Bering Coast

Your shores hide the Eskimo's past,
Covering it with sands of time.

Every once in a while,
You uncover jewels of relics,
As if to remind the world
That once, in times past,
Eskimos shared the shore with you.

When I was nine,
I walked your shores
Nearly every day.
Once, I found a baby seal.
When I approached,
It looked at me
With tears in its eyes.

The Eskimo in me said,
"Take it for its fur and liver."
The child in me said,
"I need to care for it."

Eskimo,
   Seal,
      Together a culture.
So interwoven like braided hair,
Shedding the same kind of tears.

The child in me carried the seal
And it disappeared off the Bering Coast.
The Eskimo in me went with it.

A Lone White Arctic Owl

A lone white arctic owl flying
in the moon-lit night, searching
for tundra critters for dinner.

A lone white arctic owl wondering
what he would see tonight.

A lone white arctic owl ever
alert for movement on the tundra.

A long white arctic owl sees a
young Eskimo male wandering
aimlessly.

A lone white arctic owl watches
this warrior of the tundra.

A lone white arctic owl sees the Eskimo's
agony, pain, and despair.

A lone white arctic owl tries to understand
this Eskimo's feelings of uselessness.

A lone white arctic owl notices a liquor
bottle in the Eskimo's hand.

A lone white arctic owl eyes, huge bulging,
cries for the Eskimo.

A lone white arctic owl witnesses another
tragic, useless death on the tundra.

A lone white arctic owl flies on and on
tears freezing before they hit the tundra.

Gaslight

"Yes, what will you have?"
You want to answer
"Happiness and peace of mind."
But a voice says, "Oly."

As the evening turns to night,
You notice that the Gaslight
Becomes more crowded,
And reality farther away.

You look around at all the lonely people
Looking for other lonely people.
As the night turns to early morning,
The Gaslight becomes loud, smoky,
And the lonely people become lonelier.

"Last call—"
People yell, "No!"
"You can't let us go back to reality."
Music blares, "All the lonely people,
Where did you all come from."

You leave, knowing you'll be back,
Because the Gaslight beckons you,
    Fools you,
        Seduces you,
Drugs you into thinking
    That
        This is reality.

Charlie Blatchford

I was born at Golovin, Alaska, a small village on the Norton Sound on August 4, 1942, one of seventeen mom and pop conceived and supported through a Native lifestyle.

In the spring of 1949 my pop and brother were lost on sea ice while hunting seal. This was devastating beyond understanding for our food source had been extinguished.

Shortly thereafter an older sister living in Anchorage relocated three brothers, a sister, Mom and myself to Homer. In our Dog Skin Parkas and Mukluks we entered a new world. Learning a new language and life-style. Very Scary!

I completed grade eight, flunked number nine, ending my school education. As a young man in my twenties I traveled around the state furthering my formal education without realizing.

During my mid twenties I was wed, had two children and in 1971 I started a Roofing Company specializing in Federal contracts. In 1978, just when I smelled success I got a divorce. My business started tumbling. My downfall was introduced by booze and drugs.

Now I am, in 1990, again married to a dedicated and loving wife.

We have three lovely children. We are now residing in Unalakleet. I feel I am free of said incumbents, the liquid curse. Now I, along with many others can walk with a free Spirit.

In addition to being included in this collection, some of my poetry is in *The American Poetry Anthology*. This is a privilege to me and a hope for other aspiring Native writers.

I am first a babe in writing words. Our next generation shall blossom and expressions shall flow, announcing to the world an ancient culture adjusting finally to a new way of life.

I thank you, Mom and Pop, and I hope with pride you are looking down.

Why?

Storms of passion,
flow through my mind.
Glad and sad
good and bad,
consume me.
I am Eskimo
    this is my being.
I am White
    this is not true.
I am a Shaman
    I am afraid.
I am as the wind
    being felt but not seen.
I am a father to my children
    I am at peace.
I am a husband to my wife
    her love is as my soul.
I am ME!

Charlie Blatchford   27

Magnetized

I gaze beyond my eyes
   my father is calling me
Beyond the coldness of the sea
   my father is calling me
Beyond the abundance of the sea
   my father is calling me
Beyond the fear of the sea
   my father is calling me
Beyond the understanding of the sea
   my father is calling me
Even beyond the being of me
   my father is calling me
Now I am home
I am finally home
I have answered my father
   calling me.

Forgotten Words

Our language, of what I know,
has been prepared
with wisdom and grace.
The fine skin has been fleshed
and lies to one side.
The innards have carefully
been exposed.
Their sweet flesh
ready for feast.
Meat, the staple of life,
is consumed with satisfaction . . .
Sedating our need
for new words.

Charlie Blatchford   29

Nora Marks Dauenhauer

My early childhood was a traditional Tlingit way of life. We lived on a boat most of the year, except when we stopped in Hoonah where we lived in my father's clan house and visited my uncle's clan house. When we stopped in Juneau we stayed at my grandfather's land at Marks Trail. Our home language was Tlingit, and only when we were in Juneau and had to make business deals did any of our family members speak English. Our way of life included traditional Tlingit foods. Some were made at dryfish camp, and others we gathered during their seasons. We lived on game meats most of the time. We bought only staple food from the stores in the towns where we stopped for fuel and to buy supplies and sell fish or furs.

I started school when I was eight years old, and attended periodically until I dropped out at sixteen. At eighteen I married and raised four children from whom I have thirteen grandchildren. When my children were raised, I completed my GED, went on to college, and received a BA in anthropology. While formal schooling was not a priority in our family, Tlingit education was very important. This was the responsibility of each member of the family. Everyone in the family was a storyteller. Also, each person had an expertise in art and traditional technology which they taught to the children. There was always instruction on how to be a good human being.

I have tried to write from this sense of place and self. My writing is greatly influenced by my research in Tlingit language and literature. It is always exciting to work with elders from different areas and with different experiences. I try to listen to my thinking and thoughts of old and new things. Influences other than these are my colleague, co-author, and husband Richard Dauenhauer, a former poet laureate of Alaska, who gives me support and a sense of comradery. Other influences come from my family, and from my reading of Native American and Asian American literature, as well as some of the classics of Western literature. At this time of my life I feel an urgency but I'm not always sure for what. I know I would like to write more.

Raven, King Salmon, and the Birds

a play based on Raven Stories by
Katherine Mills
and George Davis

First performed September and October 1989,
Juneau, Washington, and Oregon
by the Naa Kahidi Theatre
Sealaska Heritage Foundation

Characters:

> Story teller
> Raven
> King Salmon
> Robin
> Chickadee
> Steller's Jay
> Magpie
> Snow Birds
> Small Song Birds
> Skunk Cabbage

Certain lines are spoken by the entire cast in Chorus.

Props:

> Plastic club or long balloon, stump, greenstone
> Salmon may be either a prop or character

Music:

> Raven Song (Du Yaa Kanagoodi)

SCENE I
Beach in Southeast Alaska

Story Teller

Raven: walking along a beach.
He sees a King Salmon
jumping out of the water.

Chorus (as Salmon jumps)

Ei, haaw! Ei, haaw! Ei, haaw! Ei, haaw!

Story teller

He stared and stared,
hungrily.
Raven hadn't eaten for days.
He could hear his stomach growling.
    [Raven makes sound of stomach rumble.]
He could almost taste the salmon.
He thought,
"How could I get the salmon
to come in?"
Then he found a Greenstone.
He brushed it off
and turned it this way and that way.
An idea!
"I'll put this up on a stump!"
Then Raven said,
"Hey, you! You dirty guy!
Listen to what this Greenstone
is saying about you.
Hey, you!
Listen to what he's saying!

Chorus

Ei, haaw! Ei, haaw! Ei, haaw! Ei, haaw! Ei, haaw!

Story teller

King Salmon jumped out there.
Raven: yelling at the Salmon,
"Hey, you!
Listen to what this little green stone

is saying about you.
Listen!"
King Salmon jumped out there,
out from the beach Raven was on.

Chorus

Ei, haaw! Ei, haaw! Ei, haaw! Ei, haaw!

Story Teller

Raven starts yelling insults.
"Hey, you!
Listen to what Greenstone said.
Come on ashore!
Come, jump on the beach!"

Chorus

Ei, haaw! Ei, haaw! Ei, haaw! Ei, haaw!

Story Teller

And King Salmon
jumped up on the beach.
Raven,
in his foolishness,
and short-sighted exploit,
forgot he should have a club
to hit the nose
of the King Salmon.
So he told the King Salmon,
"Oh, my! Pardner,
let me go in the woods first.
I can hardly stand it!"
So he ran up in the woods
to get a club.
When he came back down,
he had his club.
But the King Salmon
was out in the bay again,
jumping around.

Chorus

Ei, haaw! Ei, haaw! Ei, haaw! Ei, haaw!

Story Teller

He jumped out there.
Raven: "Hey!
Listen to what the Greenstone
is saying about you!
You dirty mouth!
You dirty-gilled person, you!
Hey! Do you hear this?"
Salmon jumped out there,
not bothered.

Chorus

Ei, haaw! Ei, haaw! Ei, haaw! Ei, haaw!

Story Teller

Raven: "Here's what he just said.
You dirty spined salmon."
At this the salmon
jumped on the beach
by Raven.
As it jumped on the beach
Raven attacked it
with the club.
He slammed the club on its nose
again and again and again and again
until it was gone.

SCENE II

Story Teller

The salmon was too heavy for him,
so Raven organized

a group of birds
called Alaska Native Birds.
Their acronym
is ANB.
Raven said to them,
"Hey, Grandchildren.
Help me pull this salmon up,
and we'll bake it."
When they pulled it up, Raven said,
"We have to dig a pit for the salmon."
They dug up a huge pit.
Then Raven said, "Gee!
Now we gotta get some skunk cabbage
to wrap our salmon with,
and so we can put some skunk cabbage
on the bottom of the fire pit.
Why don't you go and get some?"
Birds: "Let's pick only the nice ones.
That guy is a nice guy."
They went and picked nice huge ones,
nice clean ones,
and hurried back with them.
Then Raven asked them,
"Let me see."
They piled them up in front of him.
Then he looked them over.
While he looked them over
he asked,
"Where did you pick them?"
They all pointed to the same place
behind the village.
Raven exploded,
"Yuck! Yuck! Yuck! Yuck!
It's contaminated there!
It's as bad as PCBs.
When my wife was alive
she used to go over there!
Throw them away!
They're not fit
to wrap the salmon in!
Throw them away!
Throw them away!

Look at the brown spots on them!"
He was pointing to imaginary spots on them.
The little birds were sad
but they still wanted to help Raven.
Birds: "We'll get better ones,
and clean ones too."
Raven told them,
"Go over two mountains.
Get the skunk cabbage
only from there."
Birds: "How could we know
that his wife used to go there?
We should have asked."
They left.
Birds: "Let's hurry.
Salmon is fresh
for only a while."
They hiked.
In the meantime
Raven put the layers of skunk cabbage
and the salmon over them
on the bottom of the pit
the birds had dug for him.
He covered it
and built a fire over it.
When it was done
Raven ate
to his heart's content.
Once in a while
he would burp a long one.
You see,
it's ok to burp
at a Tlingit dinner.
So he ate and ate
and burped and burped
until he ate up
the whole salmon
("Oops! I ate it all!")
before the birds could have any.
He was content.
All that was left was the tail.
He put his craft to work.

He tried to roll a stump
over the fire.
He couldn't.
So he finally just stuck
the tail under it.
He said
"There!"
When the birds came back
Raven was sitting
by the uprooted tree stump
looking sad, and saying,
"We're so unlucky, you guys!
This tree stump
rolled over on the salmon
on the fire
and we can't even salvage
any of it!
We've lost all of it!
It's all gone!
All the skunk cabbage
were brought for nothing."
Only the tail
was sticking out
from under the stump.
The birds were sad.
They cried.
The birds were wailing.
All the birds were crying
"Waaaaaaaaaaa!"
Some were angry.
Raven was in a fix.
He thought,
"What am I going to do?"
An idea!
Raven: "Hey! You guys!
Why are you crying?
Come here!"
Robin came over.
Robin was cold
and got too close to the fire.
When his belly caught fire
he didn't even feel it

until it was red.
Robin: "Ouch! I'm burning!"
Chickadee was crying.
She rubbed her eyes.
She was so upset while she cried
she rubbed her eyes
and the top of her head.
She rubbed in the soot
she had all over her
from the ashes she was sitting in.
"I'm tired and hungry," she said.
Bluejay was so angry she went on
"Yakidi, yakidi, yakidi, yakidi, yak!
You should have cooked the salmon
more carefully!
You should not have built
the fire there
near the stump!"
Raven pulled the Bluejay's feathers
around his head
into a topknot
or a bow.
Raven: "You shouldn't be sqwaking!
Look at what a nice looking guy you are!
You look funny angry!"
Magpie was trying to fly off
but Raven pulled him back
and tried to calm him down
by running his claws
down his tail.
That's why Magpie
has a forked tail.
This is where the chickadee
got its black top
and black rings around the eye.
Robin burned her belly
trying to get at the fire.
Blue jay still has the comb
Raven made for him
and is still angry
he didn't get any salmon.
What happened to Raven?

After he smooth-talked
the Alaska Native Birds
he realized he had been so busy for so long
he worked up an appetite.
You could hear his stomach growling.

Chorus

Growllllllllll!

Story Teller

He quickly grabbed
the King Salmon tail, and said,
"I think I'll go see
my brother-in-law, the Brown Bear."
And he flew away.

Chorus

Raven song: du yaa kanagoodi.

Chilkoot River / Lukaax̱.ádi Village

After the bulldozer
went through the village
site,
no one bothered to look
to see
if they had uncovered anything of
significance.
They left
where they uncovered a grave
site.
The skull facing the road seemed
to say,
"Look at me, Grandchild.
Look at what is happening to me."

Spring

Skunk cabbage
punching through the ground,
punching to spring.

Willie

When I talked to you
in the hospital,
after recovering from pneumonia,
you said to me,
you were ready to go. "Don't worry, daughter,
I will be like X̲akúch' when the octopus
came up under him."
I was lost,
adrift on an ocean of tears
with no solid land
to beach my boat.

(11-24-88)

A Poem for Jim Nagataak'w (Jakwteen)
My Grandfather, Blind and Nearly Deaf

I was telling my grandfather
about what was happening
on the boat. My father
and his brothers were trying to
anchor against the wind
and tide.

I could smell him, especially
his hair. It was a warm smell.
I yelled as loud as I could,
telling him what I saw.
My face was wet from driving
rain.

I could see his long eyebrows,
I could look at him and get
really close. We both liked this.
Getting close was his way of
seeing.

(5-14-87)

Salmon Egg Puller – $2.15 an Hour

You learn to dance with machines,
keep time with the header.

Swing your arms,
reach inside the salmon cavity
with your left hand,
where the head was.

Grab lightly
top of egg sack
with fingers,
pull gently, but quick.
Reach in immediately with right hand
for the lower egg sack.
Pull this gently.

Slide them into a chute to catch the eggs.
Reach into the next salmon.
Do this four hours in the morning
with a fifteen minute coffee break.

Go home for lunch.
Attend to the kids, and feed them.
Work four hours in the afternoon
with a fifteen minute coffee break.
Go home for dinner.
Attend to kids, and feed them.

Go back for two more hours,
four more hours.
Reach,
pull gently.

When your fingers start swelling up,
soak them in epsom salts.
If you didn't have time,
stand under the shower
with your hands up under the spray.
Get to bed early if you can.
Next day, if your fingers are sore,
start dancing immediately.
The pain will go away
after icy fish with eggs.

(5-18-88)

Listening for Native Voices
(Native Writers' Workshop, Nome, Alaska)

— for Joy Harjo

Trapped voices,
frozen
under sea ice of English,
buckle,
surging to be heard.
We say
"Listen for sounds.
They are as important
as voices."
Listen.
Listen.
Listen.
Listen.

—April 14, 1984

Jim Ruppert

Robert H. Davis

Writing comes from one's particular experiences and involvement in his world, from one's participation in his unique history.

I was born in Southeast Alaska in 1954. My father was a Tlingit teacher from the Native village of Kake. My mother is a white woman who came from a Michigan farming family to teach in Alaska in the 1940's. She was adopted into the Tsaagweidi clan of Kake; my matrilineal descent makes me also Tsaagweidi, Eagle moiety. My clan crest is Killerwhale. My name is X̱aashuch'eet'.

Both parents' traditional and professional backgrounds influence my ideas about learning and teaching. Conflicts arising from my dual heritage, and attempts to reconcile them, affect my views on and sensitivity to cultural stresses of indigenous people.

Some of my childhood was spent moving back and forth from Michigan and Alaska. Having lived most my life in Kake, I feel more in tune with my Native heritage, and that point of view dominates in my writing. I believe there comes a point where one must name and own who and what he is, in order to take responsibility for where his actions and attitudes are coming from.

I am a Neo-traditional artist/storyteller. Neo-traditional, in that I believe in the continuous creation theory: everything is in perpetual renewal. Tradition and ritual are re-enactment or reproduction, and they are accurate, hardly variable, because they are intended to re*call*. They are connections to the past. They are necessary because they ground us and affirm who we are in relation to where we have been. But we are more than just our pasts. We are also reactions to the immediate present; we require rituals for contemporary themes. Form and content of older ritual are modified as they accommodate newer circumstances: the 'warrior' mentality and associated rituals are now acted out on basketball courts; secret societies and their exclusivity are enacted behind closed offices in new Native corporations. Artists and writers are using the old forms, (in new variations) to address contemporary social issues. In this way, the old and the new become one thing in the present.

This past year I have narrowed down to one dominant theme, what I, as a contemporary Native, feel compelled to express over and over in order to get beyond it: GRIEVING LOSS. As a people, we experience loss brought on by greater outside forces – relentless change, government subordination, painful acculturation and assimilation; feelings of not belonging, of being severed from a past, from a tradition, from an identity. These are but a few examples of loss we commonly experience. If GRIEVING LOSS is going to be a recurring theme in Native life (and it is), we are going to require a healing ceremony or ritual to PROCESS our grief, because unprocessed grief becomes acted out in social illnesses.

The stages of a grief are: denial, anger, bargaining, depression and finally, acceptance. A person must progress through each stage completely in order to come to terms with it. It is a *healing* process by which we get from some dis-ease to something tolerable. For me, my art and writing become this ritual, this cathartic process. In it, I can name and acknowledge whatever loss or pain or grief is unbalancing me, and it is the vehicle through which I progress beyond that condition. The point is, creation is continually unfolding, and grief unprocessed and silent also continues to unfold, to taint everything, rather than dissipating.

Once, grief was expressed in songs, or in grieving ceremonies for singular kinds of grief as in a burial ceremony for a particular person. The grief that we need to process, however, is not singular nor particular. The storytellers addressed more abstract ideas and difficult issues in story, history, myth and legend. I think that one of the responsibilities of the neo-traditional story-tellers who have the versatility within the forms of songs, chants, myths and stories, to begin naming and acknowledging our grief, as a first step toward healing. Because writing is a catharsis, and healing always moves outward, to others, and finally, hopefully to the earth herself.

Saginaw Bay: I Keep Going Back

I

He dazzles you right out of water
right out of the moon, the sun and fire.
Cocksure smooth talker, good looker,
Raven makes a name for himself
up and down the coast from Nass River,
stirs things up.

Hurling the first light, it lodges
in the round ceiling of the sky,
everything takes form —
creatures flee to forest animals,
hide in fur. Some choose
the shelter of the sea
turn to salmon escaping.
Those remaining in the light
stand as men, dumb and full of fears.

Raven turns his head
and laughs in amazement
then dives off the landscape,
dividing the air
into moment before
and instant after.

He moves north, Kuiu Island, Saginaw Bay —
rain country, wind country,
its voices try to rise through fog.
The long tongue of the sea
slides beneath the bay.

Raven is taken in by it all:

sticky mudflats horseclams squirting,
rockpool waterbugs skitting,
bulge-eyed bullheads stare through shadow,
incessant drizzle hissing.
Oilslick Raven
fixed against the glossy surface of infinity.

II

The Tsaagweidi clan settled there first,
it was right. Beaches sloped
beneath canoes greased with seal fat.
They delivered the Seal People
to these same creeks
shaking with humpies and dog salmon.
Everywhere eyes
peered from woods and mist.
The berries were thick and bursting.
And always there were the roots.

They knew how to live,
by the season.
Sometimes it seemed like the center of the world,
mountains circling within reach.

At its mouth on a knoll a fortress
guarded against intruders.
They came anyway,
from the south.
A swift slave raid
destroyed the village.
The people fled every direction.

A captured shaman
tortured and ridiculed,
scalp peeled before his very people.
Through blood running in eyes
he swore revenge
and got it.

After the massacre the battered clan
collected themselves and moved north
to Kupreonof Island.
That became Kake village.
They became Kake-kwaan,

and every once in a while
one sees in his mind
Raven tracks hardened in rock at Saginaw
where Raven dug his feet in
and tugged the mudflats clear into the woods
remaking a small Nass
because he grew homesick here,
and in those moments
they felt like going back too.

III

Kake is The Place of No Rest. It is.

I've heard of men in black robes
instructing the heathen Natives:
outlaw demon shamanism,
do away with potlatch,
pagan ceremony,
totem idolotry,
your old ways.
They listened,

They dynamited the few Kake poles —
mortuary totems fell to bones,
clan indentifiers got lost in powder,
story tellers blown to pieces
settled on the new boardwalk
houses built off the ground.
In the middle of Silver Street
my aunt drove the silver spike
that sealed the past forever.

People began to talk different,
mixed and tense.
Acted ashamed of gunny sacks of k'ink',
mayonnaise jars of stink eggs.
No one mashed blueberries
with salmon eggs anymore.

They walked different,
falling all over.
A storekeeper took artifacts for credit
till his store went up in a blaze.

Grandpa went out in his slow skiff
and cached in the cliffs
his leather wrapped possessions
preserved like a shaman body
that can't be destroyed, that won't burn.

IV

Grandpa's picture hangs in the church
next to Jesus.
He was a great minister. He traveled
with the Salvation Army band,
the famous Kake band
called to Juneau
to play for President Harding.
That must have been about when?

My father as a young man
was sent away,
Sheldon Jackson Industrial School, Sitka.

They changed him.

Separated from his family
years at a time,
one of the conditions.
Punished for speaking his own language.

Robert H. Davis   53

He graduated.
he was sent off to college,
a handsome man.
A ladies' man, I've heard,
shy, sad, but likeable.
But goddamn, you had to catch him sober
to know what I even mean.

Now they say I remind them of him.
But you have to catch me sober.

V

I turn ten or fifteen or something.
Pentilla Logging Co. barges into Saginaw.
Floathouses, landing craft and cranes.
Cables to the beach anchors, cables in the woods.
Dozers leave treadmarks in mud.

Redneck rejects, tobacco spitters
drink whiskey in rowdy bunkhouses
to the end of the drawn out day,
brag how many loads, how many turns,
who got maimed, flown out,
did they take it like a man.
Climb all over each other
gawking at the spare camp women
and their minds turn to tits and ass.

Some men can't help it,
they take up too much space,
always need more.
They gnaw at the edge of the woods
till the sky once swimming with branches
becomes simply sky, till there is only
a scarred stubble of clearcut,
head without its scalp of hair.

They hire a few Indians from Kake,
what for I don't know.
Maybe it looks good,
maybe it's the stories they come with,
maybe it's just they do things so quietly.

even sit speechless
in the stalled speedboat
while high-power rifles
chip at the cliff paintings —
the circle around three dashes
warning the invaders
from the south centuries ago
who destroyed with such precision.

VI

When my uncles were alive
they crawled on their bellies
through kelp draped rocks
at Helleck Harbor, Saginaw Bay
at a tide so low
and almost remembered,

uncovered in rubble
of boulders from the cave-in,
a hundred skeletons
in armor and weaponry —
slave hunters
piling over each other,
still hunting.

VII

Because Raven tracks are locked in fossil,
clambeds still snarled in roots,
because it has been told us this way,
we know for a fact
Raven moves in the world.

VIII

The old ones tell a better story in Tlingit.
When I was small we all used Tlingit
and English at once.
Tlingit fit better.

But I forget so much
and a notepad would be obtrusive
and suspicious. I might write a book.

In it I would describe
how we all are pulled
so many directions,
how our lives are fragments
with so many gaps.

I know there's a Tlingit name for that bay,
it means "Everything Shifted Around".

I'm trying to remember
how that shaman was called.
I can't.
Except of course he was the most powerful
and I feel somehow tied to him (was he
the one wrapped in cedar mat
sunk in the channel
only to reappear
at his own grieving ceremony
ascending the beach at Pt. White?)
I don't know. I get mixed up.
But I know my own name,
it's connected with some battle.

Listen, I'm trying to say something —
always the stories lived through paintings,
always the stories stayed alive in retelling.

You wonder why sometimes you can't reach me?
I keep going back.
I keep trying to picture my life
against all this history,
Raven in the beginning
hopping about like he just couldn't do enough.

Raven Tells Stories

Raven, gather us to that dark breast,
call up another filthy legend,
keep us distracted from all this blackness,
sheltered and cloaked by your wing. Answer us
our terror of this place we pretend to belong;
the groping spirits we're hopeless against;
from where all this bleakness keeps rising.
We ask you only to lull us with lies,
expecting the moon attached to day
because we're your parasites
nested in feather,
we hope you'll offer
any false hope
we might conjure you back, that when
your mouth opens to tell this,
we will not notice
your tongue black,
your mouth full of shadow.

Naming the Old Woman

Why was that old woman
drawing the evening
shadows toward her like a spider?
What were those signs she wove
in dance? She wore a quarter moon
on her face, was wrapped in black
wind and feather, and lugged
a cedar bag of many masks,
many songs that reminded you
of wild animals
turning to fog and catching you.

She was carried through the wildness
of dreams. She was pulled
into the tatooed skin of the earth.
She was the crazy lady
you spent your whole life hunting,
and now in the smoke
you rake at the moon shadow
burning the other
part of itself on you,
and you can't get her out of you.

At the Door of the Native Studies Director

In this place years ago
they educated old language out of you,
put you in line, in uniform, on your own two feet.
They pointed you in the right direction but
still you squint to that other place,
that country hidden within a country.
You chase bear, deer. You hunt seal. You fish.
This is what you know. This is how you move,
leaving only a trace of yourself.
Each time you come back
you have no way to tell about this.

Years later you meet their qualifications —
native scholar.
They give you a job, a corner office.
Now you're instructed to remember
old language, bring back faded legend,
anything that's left.
They keep looking in on you, sideways.
You don't fit here, you no longer fit there.
You got sick. They still talk of it,
the cheap wine on your breath
as you utter in restless sleep
what I sketch at your bedside.
Tonight, father, I wrap you in a different blanket,
the dances come easier, I carve them for you.
This way you move through me.

SoulCatcher

Far from the scent of crackling spruce,
far from throbbing sealskin drum,
into space, into wind,
wild hair flying,
old man sings
across the endless dark;
the man who leaves himself
cross-legged, hollow and still.
Medicine man: soulcatcher.

In the short sharp ripples of firelight,
painted carvings and designs
weave and snap
on the bentwood box
holding mystical charms,
soulcatcher amulets
and magic rattle.

Animal people, ocean people:
this is how he brings them back.
The air begins to move in them.
Thick men in cedar bark clothes
Incantations. Song. Dance. Story.
He could capture your soul if he had to.

The trees know.
They know how easy it is to disappear,
how a figure slouched into fire
now wears a mask of ash and bone
in a village that feels air moving.

Drowning

We think we are safe
on this beach, in this dream,
luminescence washing the shore.
Lowtide odors, sulfur, clams, kelpbed.
We come out of the fog
to cling to this fire
and our own voices
at the edge of the woods,
at the edge of the sea,
somewhere between these two kinds of darkness.

I remember stories
of a land where drowning men go,
urged there by Land Otter People,
the Kooshdakáa.
They take you ashore, they look familiar.
The village itself looks familiar.
Not even surprised at your otter-whistle voice,
you begin to live by your one sense left, hunger.
Scour tidepools for mussels, barnacles,
the flats for clams; you crawl.
Ee! Look at you!
You wouldn't recognize yourself,
hair matted and hanging
over wild roving eyes,
lips stuck in grimace.
You stink. You sniff.
Fear comes from you.
Half-awake, waiting for light
shapes transform. Everything catches our breath.

Listen:
down there cockle shells clattering,
a low-pitched whistle
I think is calling.

Hands Moving

If all the clocks in the house stopped
the haunting mirrors still
would accuse, using the past in your eyes.
We could never go back.

Michigan farm, earth smell after rain.
Fresh cut grass, lilac on breeze.
Sheets snapping, handmade clothes.
You carry wicker basket.
Barefoot, thistle, single cricket
chirrs from birch woodpile.
Next field over, swollen cow chewing.
At dusty road end, stained glass.
Big tomatoes redden in the window.
Summer preserved on shelves
under dim basement bulb.
Unshirted figure watches
through porch door screen, then turns.

We could neither return
to the canvas fishcamp,
Tlingit village cove.
Smokehouse, wisp of alder
rising on salt air.
Handtroller drags flasher
into low red sun.
Child pulled from school
traces slugs slimy trail
across weathered boardwalk.
Low voiced men beach skiffs.
Slow time before cheap whiskey,
food dipped in seal oil then
Campfire iron pot, sweet red meat.

Small boy tugging
woman's loose wool skirt.
Wooden ladle traces circles.

Old ladies whisper.
First to take a white woman, schoolteacher.
Indian kids giggle.
Chalk scratches facts.
Smell of used books.
Flies buzz.
Rusty bell finally rings.
The man at the door is both fisherman and teacher,
he goes back and forth. He hardly talks.
Even then, could they have seen it —
a dark eyed boy bent over desk
staring at the hands
telling time two different ways?

Josephine Huntington Fields

I was raised in Huslia, a small Athabascan village located in interior Alaska, until age fifteen. I left to attend a government boarding school (Mt. Edgecumbe High) and now live in an Inupiaq community, Kotzebue, located on the Seward Peninsula.

In 1983, I graduated from the University of Alaska Fairbanks with a BA in Sociology and minor in Business Administration. Presently, I manage a cultural heritage tourism operation for NANA (Native regional corporation for northwest Alaska).

I started writing for the first time this winter, when I took courses in poetry and technical writing. I loved it! Although I am 44 years old, I intend to apply to graduate programs in writing and use my MA or MFA to teach in Alaska.

The Art of Beadwork

Mother strings bright glass beads
across golden tanned hide
in small loops of three
perfectly formed circles and lines.

The scents of K'etodeetluh
and "Evening in Paris"
fragrantly mingle and drift
Reminds me dances New Year's Eve.

Her brown fingers move deftly
following small dots of ink
traced from patterns pin pricked
on sheets of umber paper.

Single strands of indigo
border petals lustrous blue
three rows from flower's center
forms pistils and the vein.

Cranberry and brilliant pink
wild roses in the making
Petal by petal, stems and leaves
slipper tops for Papa's feet.

She hums softly as she works
tunes she heard on the radio
"Hill Billy Music," she called it
Songs of lost love and pining.

Porcupine Earrings

Standing at the podium
a sea of faces before her
she looked into their deep brown eyes
and smiled.

Young women in a group
filled rows near the front
Their conversations stopped
They leaned forward in their seats.

She spoke on the merits
of the Native leaders
Such honors she bestowed
on all those men with titles.

She spoke of roles for women
Stand behind the men
slabs of concrete and steel beams
upon which great cities are built.

Like a fish out of water
sounds bubbled in my throat
Lowering my vision, I noticed
my knuckles white as pearls.

A notebook tight to my chest
I slipped through a sea
of black hair and porcupine earrings
in search of better ideas.

Snapshots in Tin Cans

Sun streamed through the window
We sat on a blanket of granny squares
From under the bed she pulled a box
tins once filled with fruit cake.

"You like old pictures?" she asked
"I'll tell you who they are"
Popped the lids revealing
rays of light on silver halide.

A man with a crooked smile
"Poor thing," she said, "he was found
lying in his wooden sled."
How his team of dogs, in unison, howled.

Now the silhouette of a low flat skiff
sits against a late day sun
children holding long thin sticks
with lines that drooped and sank.

"Reminds me of little Lincoln
He fell overboard and almost drowned."
Forgetting we had told her the story
how his hair broke water and fanned.

A circle of faces reflected the bonfire
framed by two blank coffee cans
A boat ride on the Hogotza
"We had stopped for tea," she said.

Tin by tin we worked our way
through bits and pieces of her past
A life with lonhna saggan'a
graced like the beaded cross
on the head of her bed.

Josephine Huntington Fields   69

The Other Side of Amber

A lovely village without spirits
each winter melting into spring
Springs growing hot with summers,
summers shedding golden leaves.

Homes filled with cooking smells
Mothers' sourdough hot cakes
feasts of fresh caught salmon
Endless tasks done with care.

Fathers swinging heavy axes
stretching fur pelts in the sun
These they sold for grubstake
Men of independent means.

Children playing "Andy Over"
Wildly running through the streets
Eyes like stars on winter nights
Foster homes were foreign words.

A charming village without spirits
each winter thawing into spring
Springs blossoming with summers
Summer greens turning gold and red.

We forget and drums grow silent
Amber flows in polluted streams now
Only echoes of merry laughter
will be our legacy.

Rose Atuk Fosdick

I am Inupiaq Eskimo, born and raised in Nome, Alaska located on the Seward Peninsula. My parents are both from Wales, Alaska. They moved to Nome by skinboat before I was born. They stopped a long the way, wintering at Sinrock, where my older sister was born. I was the fourth one in our family to attend college and the second one to earn a bachelors degree. Although I enjoy writing it is rare that I write to produce a creative piece. For several years I wrote in a journal which I intend to give to my son, sort of as a history of our family and his early life. I have yet to pick it up again. I heartily encourage others to write their life stories or legends down, for future generations to appreciate. There are those who hunger to write and those who think about writing and then there are those like me who accidently write something publishable.

Chicken Hill 5/20/87

There is a small hill just outside of Nome which is more like a bump on the ground than a hill. You can hear the birds and you can also hear the powerplant. We're by ourselves, three sisters, and it's good to be free. We cross a stream to get to Chicken Hill. But first we look through brush to see if there are any robins' nests. "Don't breathe on the eggs," Alice says, "the mother won't come back if you do." So we look inside a nest and count the eggs, imagine that the eggs contain miniature robins. Then on to the hill. There's old mining equipment and tunnels and cars to explore. It's never boring and we forget the time, until our stomachs say it's time to eat.

Today I drive by and the hill is covered with dog houses, the three wheelers zoom up and down on new trails. The birds and flowers are still there but are invisible as we hurry by.

Cape Nome 5/22/87

Below Cape Nome, we would set up berry picking camp every fall with Grandma. Grandma's tent would be next to ours. She would be the first to wake in the morning impatient to start picking. The soft sound of early morning waves could be heard along with the call of birds heading out to sea. We would wake up to the smell of pancakes and coffee and there would be Mom sitting next to the wood stove cooking breakfast. The sun would be shining, making the white tent twice as bright. The early morning breeze would make the tent door flap open and shut and billow the tent.

Grandma would scold all of us including Mom for being so slow and then giving in to her impatience she would begin the long walk to where the berries were. Eventually we would follow behind her. I can see her walking ahead wearing kuspuk, rubber boots, Eskimo backpack and carrying a walking stick.

Nome Seawall 5/23/87

When times were tough, or so they seemed then, I would escape to the seawall at Nome. All other noises of life would be washed out by the sound of pounding waves on the two ton rocks. Blue grey water moving to the shore in steady rhythm and then exploding on the rocks with fine salty spray covering my face. My mind would wander; were there people on the other side of the ocean? I imagined whales, walrus and seals moving through the depths of the sea. I saw seagulls fishing. The sea smelled cold and like the sea, salty. I sit back.

Roy N. Henry

I enjoy listening to the elders of my father's people talk of times when living was not the way it is now. I feel that sharing what I have experienced in hunting will allow others to realize why Alaska's Natives as a whole wish to maintain tradition and its values. However, it will only be time alone which will tell how the Inupiat are left after this "second discovery" of our lands.

I try to share my views with a friendly spirit and with lots of openness. I enjoy writing, but I have a strong tie with the ways of harvesting in the tradition style of my elders and I will gladly do that before I sit down to write.

Brevig Mission

We hunted those grounds
Those boys and I
Waded through Qingaaq
Slept in Piktaalgzhuk
And paddled through Evvalgzhuraaq

Rubber boots never helped
We slept close for warmth
Attu, he always worked the oars
Yes, I know those grounds

Tundra Bunnies

When she bends forward
    with spread knees
    to gather berries

Squats softly
    to pick the wood

While she kneels
    digging deep for roots

And hunches
    to pluck the bush's leaves

Wherever I see her
    expertly cleaning
    the fish

Or tanning
    freshly caught hides

I become jealous
    of times long gone
    when she was
    clad only in furs

Eġġalugvilik

Musk oxen come in the spring
    for protection of their young
Salmon speed through the water
    as hawks try to catch them
Lone reindeer seek refuge from bears
    wanting to eat
Geese and cranes come to rest
    and feed before moving on
        to lay eggs in the mountains a few miles away

Inuit comb the low tide beaches
    for artifacts in the summer
Mothers pick the greens of the bushes
    while the children play
        as ducks and ptarmigan squabble nearby over
            territory
        which become scarce as eggs hatch and insects
            are sought
        from stale water and the marshes which are
            treacherous

Sea gulls gather on hills nearby
    to feast on huge salmon berries
Birds of all kinds pick and pluck
    blue and black berries
Sprigs and oldsquaws fatten
    on worms and fish
        at the mouth of this stream which widens each
            new fall

Rabbits scurry through gullies to paw now frozen
 grass
Moose browse
 and seek the warmth of bushes
 which are now a little thicker
From another year of life on Eġġalugvilik
 named after all the fishes which spawn here

Willow

A bright red fox came to sniff the mossy ground.
Leaves rustled as the branches swayed in the wind.
Flowing east winds kept the buzzing insects away.
The cold nose tickled at the bark,
As it smelled the acrid odors left two days ago.
After eating lemmings and four ducklings,
The fox watched the branches sway and became
    drowsy
And fell asleep in a depression of leaves and flowers.
To squash the fleas the fox rubbed on the trunk of the
    bush,
After defecating on a clump of moss, grass, and mud
As it did two days ago when it pissed on me
Before going off to hunt small animals.

Killer Pack

Huge black and streamlined bodies
    with white patches
Sliding out of the ocean in graceful motion
    slithering onto the ice cake

Where walrus seek refuge
    having nowhere else to go
Awed at the ferociousness
    the sows watch as young are bitten in two

Ivory slashes
    sinking into cold, thick meat

The killer whales
    heave walrus after walrus
Into water where others wait
    swallowing anything bloody

Inuit

Illait maggua issimaaguzhut
Taimana illit

Illait tapkuak taimanasimaaġuzhut
Taimana issimaqliuqtut

Pinnananguaġuzhut illait
Izumaaluguuzhuat
Taimanasimaqlit

Sukshuanaqpaktuam Innukmin
Quainaqpaktuam aa
Sukshuanangaami aa
Tuk liuqtuk tamaani illaatni
Quinnaqpakliuqtut Inuit

Pinnanaqpakguzhuat illait
Nangiksimmaaqliuqtut
Tapkuak issimaaguzhuat
Tuġġuliuġak Quainaqpaktuam
Taimana illit

The People

"Inuit" translation:

Some people are this way
Let it be

Some people want to be this way
Let them be

Some people are no good
They think they are
Let them stay that way

Some real big man
A real happy one too
With another reputation also
Will come here someday
The people will rejoice

Those people that are no good
Will suffer greatly
For doing others wrong
The Great Happy Man will do away
              with these people
Let it be so

Andrew Hope, III

Andrew Hope, III is a member of the Sik'naχ.ádi (Grindstone people) clan of the Eagle/Wolf moiety of the Tlingit Indians of the Northern Northwest coast. He was born on December 23, 1949 in Sitka, Alaska, home of his father's people, the Kiks .ádi clan of the Raven moiety of the Tlingit. He edited *Raven's Bones*, (Sitka Community, 1982), a collection of writings on the tribal cultures of the Northern Northwest coast.

He founded Raven's Bone Press in 1985. Raven's Bones Press has published *Soul Catcher* (1986), a collection of poetry by the Tlingit poet Robert Davis; and *Raven's Bones Journal* (1986), an anthology of writings on contemporary Alaskan tribal issues.

He has been a member of the Board of Directors of the Before Columbus Foundation since 1985. He currently resides in Juneau, Alaska with his wife, Sister Goodwin and their two sons, Andy IV and Ishmael.

Dancing Toward the Sun #1

Tlingit
Kaach.adi man
Cast out from his people
For loving his uncle's wife
He went toward the interior
Way up from the coast
High plains
Stikine River
He came upon what he thought
was steam rising from the shore
of a frozen lake
It was smoke
Taaltan camp fires
Interior Athapascan tribe
     Sun coming up
     Hearing the drum
     Taaltan people dancing toward the sun
     Watching
     Not believing
     Shaking
     His mind started going
     Praying
     Taaltan people dancing toward the sun
     Taaltan people dancing toward the sun

Subsistence #2

Dog salmon colors
Glistening
Evening sun
Incoming tide
Washing the beach
Dog salmon shine
Silver purple flash
Reaching
Lifting a big one
By the tail
Incoming tide
Washing the beach
Time to eat
Fried dog salmon
For dinner

September 9

That Pyramid moon
That September blue
That dark night crow
That buoy flash
That beach mud
That dead humpie
That fireweed seed
That fall coming soon
For that
For it
Awé
Awé

Edgar Jackson/Anawrok

I am Inupiat Eskimo from the village of Unalakleet, on the Norton Sound Coast of Alaska. I was raised by my grandfather, Oliver Anawrok, and under his teachings I learned the traditions of my people, which I try to keep alive in my writings.

Currently I am living in Fairbanks, Alaska, and working for the

Fairbanks Native Association, Inc., as a grants writer. I'm also a student at the University of Alaska, Fairbanks.

Publications: Poems in the following anthologies: *The Clouds Threw This Light*, edited by Phil Foss, Institute of American Indian Arts Press, *Alaska: Voices from the Inside* published by the Alaska State Division of Corrections, *In The Dreamlight: 22 Alaskan Writers*, B. Hedin, Ed. Copper Canyon Press. Poems in magazines including *The Prison Writing Review, New Letters, Lemon Creek Gold.* Nonfiction prose: essay "My grandfather" in *Alaska Today.*

The Sinew of our Dreams

I breathe into you
the breath that I breathe
You
have taken a part of me
that's life
Grasp onto it
like the tree that grasps the earth
Believe in it
like the spirit that lives within you
As the clock keeps turning
we will become one
like the earth and the sea
that are rooted into each other
Our life will be the same
held together by
the sinew of our dreams

Magic Word

I am an Eskimo
a human being with feelings
Therefore
I do not need magic words in my life
to bring me good will
The magic is already there
within me

A long time ago
my people lived like that
from within
They would speak to their spirits
ask them for food
clothing, shelter, warm weather
My people would chant songs
and dance to their spirits
to bring them good fortune
good weather
good hunting

The magic words came into existence
when the language was brought to them
It was just a way of explaining
the unexplainable

Among our people
the traditions we believe in
to believe in your spirit
to believe in yourself
was the most powerful magic one could have
From within
comes the strength
the courage

Edgar Jackson/Anawrok   91

to survive in a land not our own
but nature's
We believed

And that my friends
was the magic our people lived with
the only magic that kept us alive —

to believe in ourselves

Three Songs:

I.
In the mountains

You tell me
you will be leaving
and that I should follow
The directions you gave me
were spoken in silence
In the mountains it is snowing
my heart can feel the coldness
It does not matter to you
whether I find you
I think I will spend the winter
in the mountains
There
the snow will keep me warm
and I shall wait with the silence

II.
I'm coming   I'm coming

Somewhere
she is waiting
Clouds form on top the mountains
A hazy mist covers the windows
Outside the cabin I hear a cry
I could not tell
if the sound was real
but it sounded like the woman
who once held me in her arms
moaning

III.
Already I feel the emptiness

You are leaving soon
I do not know
if I will see you again
Already I feel the emptiness
In my mind there is silence
In my heart there is sadness
And my whole body aches with longing
I do not want you to leave
What will happen to me
if I cannot have you in my life?

I will be like the arctic ice
that breaks from the shore
and drifts with the current

Letter Home

Fairbanks Correctional Center
May 30, 1982

Slowly the night comes to life
in the corner of my bed
The picture of you smiles at me—
I do not know if you are thinking of me

I can hear music in the background
My heart grows sad as laughter fills the air
I cannot tell whether the laughter is real

I gather my body and walk to the window
As the darkness awakens memories
everything around me ceases to exist
There is only your face
your smile
your voice
the silence that talks to me—

The Hunter Sees What is There

the hunter squints
his eyes straining to see what he knows
is there
standing rigid
as the ice beneath him, he waits —

around him
the earth comes to life, the sun
furnishing the warmth he needs
the wind, calming the spirit within him
the ice beneath him
keeping his senses alert

the hunter sees
what is there — the seal
he thrusts the spear with the strength of his spirit
seal/ hunter
testing each other

each straining
each praying to his spirit

for one,
the journey through life begins

Self-portrait

I am Edgar, an Eskimo
a lonely hunter
no less a man —
My brown skin, scarred
has felt the biting wind
entering my soul
scattering the hate, self-pity
my pride
into a common language
the language I'm learning to speak
to trust —

I can look back
not in anger   or hate
but with respect for my people
myself
for believing in our traditions
accepting the changes
as the world passes into confusion
as we pass in silence towards freedom —

the freedom of choice

Mary Lockwood

Mary Lockwood is a woman from the arctic who was raised in Unalakleet, Alaska. She left her village in 1970 to attend UCSC, where she graduated in 1986 with a BA in Community Studies. Her thesis, "Implications of Higher Education For Native Alaskans" is in the Alaskan Resources Library in Anchorage, and at the Merrill Library at UCSC. Her articles have been published in *Matrix, Twanas, Porter Gulch Review* and *The Sun*. She is now compiling an autobiographical novel in Santa Cruz.

The Inupiaq Malemuit of the Bering Straits were living out their last traditional seasons when I was born to their community on April 12, 1952. Grandfather Nashalook was the last chief and shaman. His daughter, Helen, the last child of his second wife, fell in love with George Lockwood, the handsome adopted son of Selma and Bennijack Lockwood. They were living with Nashalook and even began a family of three children, when Dad asked Nashalook to use the property where the remains of a Russian fort sat in the middle of a large potato garden. Shortly after a little cabin was built, I was born.

The house and family grew. My parents were constantly moving about the vast and generous landscape, bringing in harvest of plants, animals and birds to feed and clothe our family.

Motors began arriving, driving away the wild creatures who used to wander into the village. Then I saw a frightening thing – a man in a suit. Just the looks of him with a rope around his neck gave me a premonition that things were going to be real bad for us. "Alaska" became a "state" and there were urgent and strange things we had to do. The Cold War brought an invasion of military equipment and men who put up a Distant Early Warning System on the top of our highest hill. The impact left a gaping hole of marriageable maidens in our tiny village – and toxic wastes that still take a cancerous toll every year.

Among the curses of being redefined as the lowest order of American society, were the regulations of hunting and gathering. The ancient rhythms of gathering were secondary to the rules of the state. Our family starved for a while. My older brother and sister were taken to Mt. Edgecumb, eight hundred miles away. They came back bitter, and I determined not to go. I worked for the missionaries in the summers so that I might live with my parents and attend their high school.

In the chaos of uprooting an aboriginal culture with one of a temperate zone, I relied heavily on the written word as an anchor to hold me steady. The whites relied on it, and I was told by those older than me that I would have to master this technique before anyone would take me seriously in my adult life. Determined and angry at the assumption that my culture was not to be taken seriously, I began my revenge by excelling in every aspect tossed to me in school. By third grade, I was doing independent studies in math, reading and art. I read voraciously, thumbing through poetry books during recess.

I wrote to express my adolescent fever to a vague audience. The purging effect was very satisfying, since there was no one else interested in forming written words to honor the magnificence I felt in the people around me. The tumult of rushing from the Stone Age into the Atomic Age in ten short years has, in the core, a genocidal intent which drove many of my contemporaries into serious self destruction.

I wrote out what was raging inside of me – getting it out, clearing out the white man's horror so that I may be able to see the magic of our beautiful country before another houseful of horrors came thundering in.

Native authors are a rare mixture, a catalyst of oral traditions that fixate word-energies from the past, present and future on to paper. The telling has the unmovable stance of indigenous lives, the criminal aspects of genocide and a forlorn, yet undeniable feature of "still being here." Native stories tell how humans are to other humans. Contemporary stories are our way of mourning heritages so badly needed today. The loss is keen for one who knows and one who has to live in a society that doesn't know what went on.

Caribou

Some of my memories get crowded like the tangle of caribou legs seen from the eyes of a ground squirrel. They hurry up on each other, big hoofs thumping on soft tundra, cutting the stems of grass and berry bushes. Antlers clatter together, shattering the dam of forgetfulness!

I see somebody far down the gravel beach – a little person, yelling, running fast, looking back and throwing a finger like a harpoon towards the distant Indian Head Cliffs. What could make him so frantic? All I could see was a mirage of waving tan and white specks warping from Norton Sound heatwaves along the coastline.

Suddenly, the drowsy dogs tied up among the big driftwood logs on the rocky beach exploded in a snarling fervor. People from our summer camp dropped things from their hands and ran up the tundra banks to look anxiously up the beach.

I scampered to a taut larger form, who yelled the word, "Caribou!" and nearly ran over me as he dashed past to get the guns in the cabin. The electrified air of an unexpected hunt jolted the dogs to a new degree of frenzy. Screams of awe from mouths that were agape rang jangling in my ears. I clasped my hands over them and ran into the cabin.

A new sound of clattering grey stones flying from the striking hoof of strong thin legs pierced the air. I ran to the window where Dad looks out to check his gill net and heard the hissing spray of ocean water as some of the big animals driven with the intent of migration pushed along the sea. In all my young years of contact with the wild arctic animals, I had never witnessed the tremendous intent of pure, strong movement as with those snorting and bawling creatures. There was no hesitation to continue, though close contact with people spelled out their doom.

There was just a few minutes to put a dash of order to the chaos. My parents were not going to let this awesome fate of caribou transit go on without some harvest!

"Let them go past!"

"Ah-Ka!" "How big and plenty they are!" They whooped and waved their arms to spook the huge animals onward . . . towards the town and their doom. Positioning themselves on the tundra bank, away from the tied dogs, breathing and sweating profusely, they found a resting post for their shooting arms.

Skittering away from the dogs, I noticed the caribou pushed the young ones in the middle of their protective pod. Time lapsed as I narrowed my eyes to concentrate on a flash of white among the jostling herd. There was a smaller caribou of pure white — an albino! I yelled and hopped in front of the window.

The caribou surged as the rifles began firing. Several fell immediately, buckling from their knobby knees, tossing a quick prayer for their speedy ending with their final moos. Their great heads tilted for a proud show of beautiful antlers as they gave up their spirits and quickly fell upon their blood pouring on the rocky beach. One struggled to get up, managing to hop on front legs, dragging a hind that would not respond. A quick aim and crack from a rifle knocked its final bravery down.

People scrambled to the spastic death throes, shooting caribou heads to end the strong surges of determined life coursing, draining on to our summer camp beach.

I was crying, torn at the caribou's magnificence and at the slaughter and noise. The air remained repercussive from the shattering of shouts, dogs barking, clattering of stones, whoops of victory.

I went outside, hurrying to see a caribou up close, I suppose. The madness was tangible.

One of Grandma Selma's Stories

One day, during the long, bright arctic summer, Grandma Selma was tending to her fire out on the beach at her summer camp. She heard a faint, strange sound that hummed constantly, and looked around. The dogs were awake and had their ears and fur standing up.

"That must be coming from my stove," she thought, and poked at the fire with a stick.

Still the sound continued; and even amplified.

She was beginning to be frightened, and the dogs paced nervously.

Further down the gravel beach, Bennijack halted his easy gait to listen. Something was different. Of all the familiar sounds, there was a new tone — and it didn't stop. He clutched his harpoon and fidgeted nervously. His sharp eyes scanned the pristine landscape of the arctic. Somewhere in the south, following the coastline, was a little speck in the sky. The reverberations grew as it became larger.

Soon it was apparent that this was the source of the intrusion into all that he knew. As the tremendous roar of the airplane engulfed him, he let out a cry and threw his harpoon up with all his might. The harpoon tangled in a propeller. Down the airplane pummelled, and with incredible explosions, crashed onto the tundra!

Paul

Paul was always late for school. We would be reciting "the Pledge of Allegiance", or taking roll call when the classroom door would creak open to show his tousled dark hair over sleepy eyes. He would stand for a moment, confused and embarrassed in full view of our sight. Momentum would lull when he trudged over to Mr. Quebbelman's desk to hand over a scrap of paper with some scrawled note from his mother—if he had one. Otherwise, he would go over to his empty desk and fit in as best as he could with our activity to wait cautiously for a reprimand.

As his classmate for three years, we bore the burden of his quaint arrival, our disapproval softened by his rough, worn clothing, his stomach rumbling from hunger and the loud thud of his huge boots which sometimes did not have socks in them. Paul's light eyes of blue blinked at the bright fluorescence of our classroom, and gave him moments when we were erased so that his shivering body could melt with the warmth in the classroom.

We would snicker at the holes in his clothes or at his large pants held up by a piece of rope. His friends, Gary and Vincent, lived at the other end of town. Over hills and vales of snowbanks developed by the east wind, they made their way in the black mornings of winter. During howling storms that rattled the huge windows of the largest building in Unalakleet, they would sometimes appear late. Their parkas dusted with frost, boots packed inside with snow, red faces hid deeply in fur rimmed hoods. Their parents or big sisters or brothers would walk over to Mr. Q's desk and explain their tardiness. With flourishes of guardians, encouragements for the day ahead and promises to lead them back home at three o'clock if the storm lasted, the older folk bade their young ones goodbye.

Sometimes Paul did not show up, and in the early moments of class we waited to hear the creak of the door-

way. Mr. Q grew more anxious as the morning went on –
because, though Paul did not live very far away, no one
took him over on those mornings of storm. There were dog-
towns and slippery snowbanks – strong gust in a blizzard
that could blow a light child out to the river or ocean . . .

During the deep part of winter Paul wore a squirrel
skin parka with rips in it and a scrawny strip of wolverine ruff around the hood. His light skin would be blotchy
red and his small hand stiff with cold as he thawed out in
the hallway. He would put his awful parka deep into the
pegs lined with our outer wear gear, for it was so
pathetic. As soon as the blizzard would pass, he wore a
short woolen black jacket, which had no hood. And he
would play out at recess warming one red ear with a
ragged mitten.

He never did well in school. He would read the primer
very slowly outloud, the tips of his ears growing red from
hearing his soft voice for everyone to listen, struggling to
form sounds roughly, as though he was learning a foreign
language. His report card was disastrous. So bad, in fact,
that Mr. Q was compelled to visit Paul's mother about
the seriousness of the situation.

With all the aplomb of an ambassador on the trail of
righteousness, Mr. Quebbelman made his way down the
short distance from school to the tiny log cabin of Mrs.
Agibinik's. In the dark one room cabin, he saw a thin
lady. A scrawny pile of driftwood beside a drum stove
was the source of warmth where beds huddled near. Mrs.
Agibinik had no husband, and an older son, "Blondie",
begotten by an Air Force man, led a secret and hostile
life away from her wretched place.

She served Mr. Q some tea with shaking hands, implor-
ing that she was the reason for Paul's poor performance
at school, that she couldn't keep the place warm, or feed
and clothe a growing boy. Her alarm clock was broken
and it was hard for her to tell the time in these dark
depths of a sunless winter.

Mr. Q left shaken at a poverty he had never seen
before. The forthrighteousness that compelled him to
teach in arctic villages in a new state of America became
inflamed at the meager ties to life his student had just a
stone's throw away from his own secure home.

He began to attend our church and give generously in the offering plate. He visited other homes to tell our parents about the availability of welfare. He came back with clothes or blankets and listened more openly to our voices.

It was during this time that he began to confront the diversity of students in the class. There were three sections, Group A, who progressed without hindrance; Group B, the normal set of students, and Group C, Paul's group, who were slow.

During reading classes, I walked quietly to a table in the back of the classroom to find my place in the SRA files. I would pass Paul's desk and see the painful efforts he made in writing, twisting the alphabet into weird resemblances of the ones on the chalkboard.

Paul was happier now than in the years I had known him. He had a cap with flaps over his ears and forehead and warm sweaters and socks. Mr. Q invited him to lunch, and gave Paul his best meal of the day. With all this attention, Paul began to look at us in the eyes and we included him in some of the fun of tag and jokes.

Mr. Q also softened as Paul's smiles widened, but there was a secretiveness, too. Mr. Q was impatient with his surprise around Christmastime. He even announced that Paul should stay after school when everyone else was dismissed. Something important was in the air.

We learned later that Mr. Q had a pair of hockey skates to give to Paul. He was so happy. Paul tried them on the same afternoon in the slough that is our harbor. He skated and fell down and skated again until his little bones got tired and he wanted to go home.

About this time, the tide had risen, pushing the pan of river ice up from the shore. As arctic children, we learned from older folks to always look out for the tidal change, but Paul had no one to tell him. I suppose that once Paul noticed the increased separation of river ice to the shore, he went straight to the riverbank. A new gloss of ice had formed over a fishing hole that was partially covered by blowing snow. Paul couldn't see this in the dimming light and broke its support. He threw his remaining weight flat, spreading the top part of his body on the crackling ice and cried when he felt the whip of freezing water on his ankles pour into his new ice skates.

Some man heard his cry and rushed to the slough to investigate and help. He saw Paul halfway in the ice and tried to reach him, but a wet cold gulf from the rising tide was too much to cross. He told Paul to stay there and hold on tight because he was going to get a rope. But, when he got back in the deepening sunset, Paul was gone.

It was completely dark when the church bells rang crazily, alerting the village to a tragedy. In alarm, we looked up from our soup. The older folks left immediately, and I felt scrambled; shall I finish my soup, think of who's doing the dishes, worry about my younger brother's and sister's fear and excitement? I had a searing need to get out of the house. Suddenly, a kid tore into our house saying that Paul had fallen through the ice, and people were going out to the rivermouth with long poles to try and snag his body.

That did it, I grabbed whatever shoes and jackets and went into that black night, passing the porch light of the church and dark figures all heading to the south end of town. Some carried long poles, others lanterns, and some like me — just a flurry of trauma. I saw Mr. Q's unmistakable overcoat spreading like some huge bird's as he rushed into the darkness, past Mrs. Agibinik's and on to the rivermouth.

I was compelled by the movement and orangeness of Paul's mother's rustic cabin . . . I had never seen so many people there! Mrs. Agibinik was surrounded by people milling around — there was light all over the place! People who never gave her the time of day were waiting on her. Our preacher giving her the assurance of God . . . food, good healthy native stuff coming in bounds . . .

Transfixed, I watched Paul's mother from the snowbank. Then I heard cries from the rivermouth. Mr. Q, with his odd Russian hat and New York overcoat held the drowned body of Paul. The new hockey skates were shyly crossed over one another, swaying to the rhythm of Mr. Q's slow gait. Water poured from Paul's clothes wrapped in gunny sacks, down the skates, freezing in icicles which bent like the Grim Reaper's fingers towards our Germanic teacher who pressed on to the red wail of Paul's mother.

Starbear

Dear Marie,

A bit of native culture surrounded me this month. Gerald Vizenor awarded N. Scott Momaday a Native American Literature award. I was invited to the Chancellor's Reception before the ceremonies where I talked with N. Scott about my writings – how I want to begin from as far back as I could, like Henry Tyler suggested, and keep this anchor steady throughout the telling. I told him how we Arctic folk knew there was magic in words – and he started and gave me a sharp look. Later on, while he was reading those beautiful passages in his new book, he kept looking at me, like he wanted to be sure I got the messages. Here was a vast giant of literature reading in deep tones the details of an Indian Woman's beauty. On and on until you wanted him to stop; until there were no more defenses, until you stood in front of great beauty with a bowed head – he took you there.

I bought two books of his, *House Made Of Dawn*, which David read in four or five days, and *The Way To Rainy Mountain*, which I read just a little bit before collapsing at Momaday's literate power. I'm all right, but the first pages tore away a mountain of forgetfulness fallen over my cave of infancy.

Marie, how do I tell you? How quickly I arrive at the difficulties of my task and art! Yet, somehow, I must say . . . Let me get over this notion of fear, first. I once wrote that I was afraid of being bright in beauty – that I may die from the blaze. So, I cut it short when I felt that incredible glow emanating. I saw firsthand that this is not so when N. Scott blazed to great heights proudly and loudly and didn't flame out to a pile of cinders. He was showing me a way.

In T*he Way To Rainy Mountain*, each sentence takes me a step along . . .

He said who he was – "Tai-Me", Kiowa for "Rock Tree

Boy." Rock Tree is what Kiowans call Devil's Tower, and is considered a sacred place. As an infant, he was brought to that place and given that name. A place that is the end of his people's migration.

Their legend for that great and unusual place is as follows; using his words.

"Eight children were there at play, seven sisters and their brother. Suddenly the boy was struck dumb; he trembled and began to run upon his hands and feet. His fingers became claws, and his body was covered with fur. Directly there was a bear where the body had been. The sisters were terrified; they ran, and the bear after them. They came to the stump of a great tree and the tree spoke to them. It bade them climb upon it, and as they did so it began to rise into the air. The bear came to kill them, but they were just beyond its reach. It reared against the tree and scored the bark all around with its claws. The seven sisters were borne into the sky, and they became the stars of the Big Dipper.

From that moment, and so long as the legend lives, the Kiowas have kinsmen in the night sky."

There is great happiness for me in the beginning. I love to side up to the image of eight native children playing. How fun and lively, surrounded by girls . . . teasing and testing the boy, maybe.

But, quickly, something huge and awful comes over the native boy. Could it be rage at teasing? Something beyond nature, out of control, beyond understanding!

His speech left him. He changed that way. His voice was taken, rendering him dumb. He could not communicate because of the change.

In the story, I saw my own fear, of my own brother's rendering to an animal state from an outside force, bigger than anything imaginable. I have always thought that I didn't know the native man beyond childhood companions. Something occurred to my brothers past the liveliness of playing—an irrevocable movement we were all caught up in—towards adulthood, There was a gulf coming on, separating the boy-brothers to manhood from we woman-sprouts.

"He trembled", for his body failed. He trembled because he was scared, for the Outside was coming in him.

There was no saving him, though my love surrounded this brother. To me, the message was an absorption of New Dictates that said he, as a native person, was ignorant and pagan. His beliefs in native ways were crushed deep inside of him. To be the adult indigenous man, continuing his culture is exactly what was being crushed. And that pressure made him angry.

His anger transformed into the most fearsome creature in our world. The bear. An angry bear. As a native boy he bore the burden of change. "He began to run on his hands and feet." His posture of standing upright was struck down. His head bowed low, facing the hurt deep inside his chest. Not able to look up into anyone's face. He saw his hands, the outside part of him; they were not swinging by his side, but flat on the ground, running uncontrollably. His hands that reach out to the bounty of the land, that once fashioned tools and used them for survival were flopping in front of him, slapping the ground — changing into claws.

Primal weapons. Carrying them along in front of him; That will show them how horrifying he is! Don't anyone mess around with him!

And then fur covered his body. The last shroud. The act is done. He is encased in fur. Just what our people in the arctic mimic, that change manifested to his muscle.

At this sacred place, which changed its name to Devil's Tower, a brother was changed to our most frightful creature. That for centuries we have tried to clothe ourselves in fur was done supernaturally to our brother at this natural monument of the Kiowas end of their migration!

"The sisters were terrified." No trust could be extended. It was shorn by the Outside change. They grouped together screaming, clustering and clinging to each other in fright. We're still doing that. As manifestations of the tremendous feminine energies of this Earth, we are at peril from the Outside changes, for "directly there was a bear where a boy had been." Our future man is not there. In its place is a creature we cannot progenate native children with — ever. What is in front of our eyes, right at the watershed of childhood, is the angry animal of the shaman! The continual prayers of damnation of the missionaries came true, for they prayed and worked so hard to their angry god. They ripped away our connection to grow up whole in our ways . . . and if we go blindly towards our love we shall surely die.

But our eyes are open, watching all of this taking place. We are still pulsing with Earth's energies, which warded off this weird changes from us. We carry the seeds of life in us, and because we do, we notice signs of danger. This is dangerous. You ask David Harrison, an Athabaskan, who has a Yaqui wife how dangerous it is to produce children that this outside world calls – "non-native".

So, we use our good legs and run. That much we can do – flee, Marie, all the time we flee from genocide. We got to do that, keep going . . . together as sisters we got to run and not get stuck because our good female native souls will get run over. Every day we got to move along, run real fast because there's a shaman's animal right on our heels that will take our nativeness away.

And I, for one, know how swift and powerful a bear moves – especially an angry one – even if it is a relation. Swifter then magic he can tear you up – more than that dreadful dream of nuclear bombs, for he is real and roaming the wilds. Those claws dig in and rip before you die. His teeth and claws roar and swipe and he puts his huge hairy head by your eyes and bites down before you die. He lets you know his anger, his raging heights of pure wildness before you get out of this body. He will bat you around helplessly and pounce on you in full rage before you are gone. You have to live a little bit when he catches up with you, you know.

"They came to the stump of a great tree."

This was what was left of a grandmother. One that lived a long, long time, roots still deep in the ground. One that had witnessed the old days, who drank good water for a long time and spread out from the blessings of the sun. So that they all were sacred friends on this earth.

Being thus connected to woman, She became alive from their danger. She always had sheltered life, so she said, "Climb on up."

Little did they know how far up they would go. Once again, the old tree rose. This time supernaturally. Because she was from the old world, growing in this new one would be different. Because of the enormous rage of the bear, she went far, far up. The bear tore at her old sides, raking deep wounds all around here. She took on the bear's rage intended for the seven sisters. That is how a woman can love. A native woman's love lifts up her little girl and shows the world her sides and the world leans on her in a terrible way. So angry, so base, defiling her beauty, throwing rage in her direction.

"The seven sisters were borne into the sky."

That's where we all begin, from the sky. It is masculine, the intellect; in the deep void, She returned us that far away to keep us safe. That's where we go for purification. Some thoughts are bright in that mystery. They are born up there. We have sisters up there. We have sisters who think clearly, with no hesitation, and they may look as different as stars are than you and me; but the good grandmother in her wisdom says, "Get up there." So we have to use our minds in their highest way to make it as good here in life.

When I close my eyes to pray, it travels up, to talk to a little light in the darkness, and then I am very honest about my heart—my heart moving about here on Earth . . . what it sees, how it is touched, how it aches and asks questions. My heart is much younger than the stars, being made of flesh and pumping around blood. I know I am returning from where I came from when I pray. And I was a bright, bright star—blinding as a baby—a baby that knew about bears.

". . . and they became the stars of the Big Dipper."

Another name is URSA major. The Big Bear Constellation. Remember the Alaskan State song? "Eight stars of gold on a field of blue, Alaska's flag may it mean to you, the blue of the sea, the evening sky, the Bear, the Dipper, shining high! The gold of the early sourdough's dreams, the precious gold in the hills and streams. Alaska's song is Alaska's dreams, the simple flag of the last frontier."

I am the Eighth star. The north star. I look at it and I will always know how to go home. I am the big sister to those seven who jumped up from the Rock Tree. I lent them this hand that writes to get them up in the sky. Grandmother knew I was there. She rose up and said, "Here! Keep them safe. Be kind to them. They are going to change and it might be strange for them. Let us save their light!"

You see, I had to be clear and strong to be a part of this. I had to go through all those trials and tribulations, with the help of every guardian to be present for N. Scott so that the legend is complete. He might have been looking at me like that during his reading because he recognized that kinship, that part of his peoples story sitting right there in that room. He, "Tai-Me", Rock Tree Boy, his grandmother, A-ho and I have existed before.

The North Star. It's also a ship that brings food every spring up the coast where I come from. In my life, all the stars on this hemisphere rotate around me. Quietly I shine as these guides go round and round in their slow beautiful dance. It takes people much longer to come around. I might tell them to wake up and quit dreaming—quit sleep-walking in delusions and listen to what I will say.

The North Star has plenty to say.

March 19, 1989

Marie, it's been three months of sobriety. Such good times! So correct not to have that killing feeling deep inside bodily tissue! I really want to thank you for showing me that way. It's truly been a blessing—and more gracious because it is a unique gift from you. Each day I am here with David is like that, too. The space and joy created seems as fragile as sobriety. I feel a new area of happiness, a new wideness—and depth too. I feel a return to those times when a person could hear and understand the language of plants, animals, rocks and water. I am far away from that lovely language, but I sense that I am coming to that direction. It feels like an ancient journey like our paleolithic ancestors who followed game across the Bering Straits land bridge. I pick up where they left off, in these modern times, in this mediteranean town of Saints on the Cross where I ended up, where we found each other. It is here I picked up a pointed hawk's feather and asked Henry Tyler to have pity on me for I had a need to pray.

I think it would be lovely to be an old Malemuit lady who listened to the voices of the land, sea and air! So craggy and old; hard to move around, smiling at the sun or rain or fog or bird's songs. I have no doubt that my sweet handsome sons will bring children over to tug on my skirts and follow me around like I used to do with Grandma. Wouldn't it be fun, Marie, to grin toothless smiles at each other, laughing croaking sounds that we lasted so long?

June McGlashan

Of herself, June McGlashan writes: "I was born in Akutan, Alaska, I have lived in the Aleutians all of my life. The Native here are Aleuts. I find the way of life here is unique. We have the most terrible weather in the state – blowing up to 100 mph during the winter at times. The Aleuts live off the sea. They are able to hunt in all types of weather; stories have been passed through villages and through generations of natives.

Not only is the weather drastic, so is the scenery. Tall mountains encircle many of the villages, making the Aleutians a picturesque place to live.

My poetry is based on my life here."

June McGlashan began writing at the early age of 16. After receiving her high school diploma in Unalaska, she attended Sheldon Jackson College and received her A.A. degree. During her time at Sheldon Jackson she worked with and knew personally such Alaskan poets and writers as John Haines, Cheryl Morse, Fred Bigjim, and Sister Goodwin. She lives in Akutan, Alaska and is the mother of two children, a boy and a girl.

Grandmama's Visit

You show me where
the ice water flows
from the stream.
This is the cold summer
water for the village.

You let me pick forbidden
rain flowers and now I
know it will rain tomorrow.
Just superstition, you say.
And lay them on the table.

And in Aleut, you have a name
for every person.
I know enough to understand
who you speak of in whispers
to the elderly.

Everyone in Akutan,
is allowed to call you
Grandma; and every hunter
knows to bring his catch
to you.

Mothers bring their babies
to you, each day.
You have the time to hold
each one.

I ask you if it is good
to be a grandmama.
You nod and smile.

Ever Have One of Those Days?

when the world seems perfect and
no one would change it for you.

To touch a chiseled mountain
and feel proud of a carved
wood seal from Snake-the-carver.

The oil stove's out of fuel,
can't cook right.
But the old man comes in
smiling and laughs.

Ever walk to the goose—
smell its burning fuel.
Let steambath smoke
blow in your face.

Dog jumps on me,
gets fur stuck over
all my clothing.
And he talks a happy bark.

Then night approaches,
My man brings in a trout
and hugs me with slimy hands.
Ever have one of those days?

The Wait

I watch the South into
the Akun Pass.
Every day, night; even
though I know it is
not time yet.

The winds begin to williwaw.
Colder snow piles on
my doorstep.
The sunrise is red.

I hang my sweater
by an oil stove.
Again it will be
warm.

The fleet arrives,
I feel forever
Each slip across the
bay. All as silent as
the other.

They say I never smile. I never
did.

Afraid

Afraid as a child,
dark attics – spider country
webs drooping in corners/
ceiling.

Afraid of sleeping in dark,
Drunks sneak upstairs,
& touch secret places.
A dog that bit my leg forever.

Afraid to die
In open sea, where
no man finds me
and rests my bones home.

Afraid to be afraid,
replacing it with
anger, resentment or
a stronger solid self.

Devil's Night

Holiday, evil day.
Men dress as creatures
of imagination
Their faces held masks,
secretly.

At night women and children
remain indoors.
If anyone dares to
go outside,
Men would frighten them.

Dances, songs of the hideous sound.
Rhyme with the evening wind.
Men return home after winds die.

Women speak of evil happenings.
Depend on men for strength and support.
The men put the spears by the door.

Thirteen Ways of Looking at the Seaotters

I – A close-up pic hung in
a crowded library.
Two seaotters with lazy eyes.
Those eyes boring through you.

II – The fattest seaotter.
With that pearly, black nose.
Stretching his tiny toes
outward.

III – The smallest seaotter,
Close beside the fatter.
Hands clench tight together,
Protect a morsel.

IV – The Aleut story starts,
The seaotter myths tell
the seaotters are born
Aleut sister and brother.

V – On the dock, in the darkness.
Walking home, watching waves.
Hearing that patter of rushing feet.
Wet, swishing, paw flippers.

VI – Mountains large, circle
Every being small.
Like the seaotter, with their
Heads popping out of the water.

VII – Their smell, best imagined,
Clean, salty, fresh and moist.
Spotless from day to day,
By the swift flow of currents.

VIII – Those beings, to be admired.
The softness, silk, shine
Priceless jacket.
Insulated with food stored warmly.

IX – Their fuzzy goblin bodies,
Dance to the crusty bottom.
Unlocking clams from kelp,
Again to nibble.

X – The Aleuts lived with the seaotters,
With the clouds, swirling of
lively, chanceful wind.
Protected to see again a hidden sun.

XI – Once in a great while,
One, with luck-two, seaotters
Drift in the blue bay.
Far out at the edge of mountains.

XII – That dusty picture,
Never dusted since it was hung,
Sloppily hung.
Dust can not be respected.

XIII – There is no thirteenth way,
Of looking at those two
Seaotters.

Whale Chief's Son

Surrounded by green wood now,
Strands of short yellow grass.
The warm breeze over the bay,
A cement walk colored gray.
Rhythm of your footsteps.

Lazy steps, calm as if
Tomorrow can wait a little longer.
Words softly spoken,
You memorize that warm wind.
Flowing words into listening spruce.

Black coal, clear alert eyes,
Reaching from your warm heart.
Back into the cloud mist.
Whales white smell.
Soaking fresh clean hands.

Old Chiefs still exist here.
Your father, a tall toned shadow.
Watch the waves endless green.
Whale out in the giving sea.
Invisible colors of memory sweep by.

Martha B. Malavansky

My name is Martha B. Malavansky. I am an Aleut/Inupiaq Eskimo who was born on November 18, 1958 on St. George Island, Alaska. St. George is one of five islands called the Pribilof Islands. These islands are 200 miles north of the Aleutian Chain and 800 miles west of Anchorage, in the middle of the Bering Sea.

I am married to Max Malavansky and we have three beautiful children. Nicole is 12, Max Jr. is 10 and Victor is 8 years old. I graduated from Mt. Edgecumbe High School when I was 16, attending the University of Alaska Fairbanks that fall, majoring in biology/chemistry. But I was too young, not really sure of my ambitions, so I dropped out of college and came back to St. George to visit my grandmother. In 1986 I decided to actively pursue my education again, and started taking a course here and a course there. It wasn't until 1988 that I realized that I was accumulating enough credits to have an Associate of Arts degree, which I received in July 1990.

I have been working for the St. George Traditional Council full time since 1984 as an Administrator, and prior to that I worked for the City of St. George as a Deputy City Clerk and part-time for the Traditional Council as a secretary and grants writer.

St. George is a beautiful island and to date we are struggling to build an economy based on fisheries. The cultural changes I have seen in the island among the people are subtle and yet still pronounced. The people my age are struggling with changes such as increased awareness of the world around them via cable television, and a decrease of interest in the Russian Orthodox religion, which has been a basis of the Aleut culture for over 200 years. I find myself torn between two worlds. I want to spend the rest of my life on St. George, but in order to finish my education I will have to leave, and there is no guarantee that I will return. I have also come to realize that I am not alone in this dilemma. A lot of other villagers in Alaska are experiencing this in one way or another.

I feel that my poetry reflects the changes I see around me, and the hope that we will be able to maintain our identity and heritage through these times.

(untitled)

The old Aleut man
sat in the rocking chair
like he had been sitting there
forever
his brown weathered face
crinkled with years
and eyes slanted from
hunting in the arctic sun
looked out to the sea

In his ageless way
he spoke
"We never complained
of nothing to do
No one worried about time
or money, there was none

"We waited out the winter
for the birth of Choochkis
arrival of the Hoolastock
the cries of the Kaheeyas
finding home in the bluffs
through blankets of fog

"All this brought excitement
and anticipation to everyone
Bellies would be filled
Now I wait for mail
watch the news
and pay for groceries
yet the Hoolastock
still come every year"

I turned, turned to look
out to the sea
in the direction he was
an old Aleut man
and a young Aleut girl
paddled out over the horizon

The Circle of Three

As a child I dreaded Easter
waking up several hours before dawn
struggling with
smaller than usual tights
twisting one leg around
a chubby ankle

Inside the church
above the old floor grates
warm air blew up my leg
making me sleepy
I felt safe

Surrounded by incense
and the joyous sound
of the choir
singing "Kristovoscrese!"
Christ is Risen!
sent a chill of excitement
down my back

Last Easter
before midnight
my daughter mumbled and cried
as she pulled on her tights
saying she would rather be home

As I stood in the choir
in my mother's place
singing 'Voeestinvostrese"
Indeed He Is Risen!
Her eyes lit up with joy
I knew we'd be safe

A Litany for Love

The night before the funeral
she didn't sleep
sitting on the edge
of their bed
bent with sorrow
she cried in the dark

All I could say was
"Everything will be okay"

She replied
"It's so hard
Why did he have to
What will I do
without him"

Time spent with him
reduced to pictures
of the last fishing season
old checkered work-shirts
size 12 boots
and a dent in the pillow
on his side of the bed

No, I don't know
if everything will ever be okay

Things I Forgot Today

I sat across from her
She talked of little things
like the fox she had fed today
She said it had been around
for some time

"Did you see the stars tonight
I whistled to see
if they would dance
They were milky

"Did you hear the snow
It's so cold
that when you walk
it crackles"

I didn't see the stars
hear the snow
feed a fox
I fed my kids
washed dishes
typed reports
did my homework

My days are full
but let me write these in
fox feeding
star watching
and walking

R. Singh

Renee Matthew

I'm an Athabascan Indian from the Interior of Alaska, and a firm believer in the need for better communication between my culture and that of the dominant society. Being raised in the village of Tanana was a wonderful experience. However, when I was seven our family moved to Fairbanks where we went through many difficult adjustments basically stemming from cultural differences.

The main reason I started at the University of Alaska Fairbanks was to help other Natives cope with culture shock, alcohol, and the stresses and strains of relocating in an urban area. It took many courses in Social Work, Political Science, and Education to finally focus my energy on English as a major, with a minor in Education.

After graduating, I hope to teach here in the interior, concentrating mainly on Native students. For this reason, I'm delighted my work has been found acceptable to publish. I believe when Native students see work by Native people published they will be able to identify with it and be more able to accept their own ideas as valid and desirable.

My husband Karm and I have three children.

Indian Summer

Bright and clear is the day,
a vague scent of cranberries   crisp
in the air. Although the leaves are turning
summer has not yet faded

We walk together
along an ancient path, following
a channel of the Yukon River.
I look for her along
a long line of people
then realizing again,
she's not here
anymore.

No talking
only the rustle of leaves   a faint cry
from a child.

No time to say I love you

Gramma Cora wasn't cuddly, she was tough
as the hide she used to sew
I would sit   listening to her stories
Gramma, her mom Jenny, and me

Thinking of them together
makes me feel better.
Breathing in cool air,
Gramma was a strong woman

She wanted me to be strong too
Looking up I see a path leading
up hill, opening onto a clearing

Renee Matthew   131

White crosses gleam in the sun
as The River flows past
cousins sing "Amazing Grace"
as village women
join in

She'll always be here with me
The wind blows,
as we turn to leave
glancing back over my shoulder
"See you Gramma"

Woodsman
The One Who Wanders

We run wild, all day
"keep still" our parents say
as they cut strips from fish
not listening
we scream away, until Gramma says
the woodsman   is near
she saw them once, screaming on a river bank
dark, hairy man-creatures

Trembling in our tent
we dare not go out, even to pee
Laughing, our parents
talk outdoors by flames
reassuring us,
they are brave.

Dim light appears, cold coals flicker out
a thin blue line, slopes along the hill
Woodsman comes   stealing
fish

dogs don't wake,   leaves
lay flat, dry sticks   don't break
willows close their mouths   watching
not whispering his presence.

Tent flaps open
turning in my sleeping bag
I see his hairy back
hurrying into the woods,

back to secret camps
where stolen children plead
to go home.

Blinking, light streams into camp
stump, gathers a mossy head
sweat trickles down its wooded back onto
rocks, boughs, limbs   suspending him up

I curl in
my Gramma knows, and smiles
letting me see
all is safe

Raven's Heart

Squatting, the girl worked swiftly
strapping poles together
measuring by hand
Shaking
although she was not cold

The swollen river
watched

> She studied her father
> asking no questions,
> knowing her place
> to sit, to learn
>
> working the raft
> to support them over lakes
> strong hands   knotted mooseskin rope
> between each pole,
> attaching it to the cross
>
> the sun reflected off her brother's shoulders
> as they hauled fish,
> her mother and sisters cutting it up
>
> Raven flew over, the sun on his back
> her father nodded smiling at
> her attempts to help
>
> She saw them all pass on
> Her husband, parents, brothers and sisters

It took one winter

Two men
came in fall
by spring her village
was dead   a sickness
no one knew

Sweat filled eyes   she stretched up
smiling at the bundle in rabbit skin
close to her, Her new baby

She named her Mindona, for morning
Light approached
Her fingers bloody, her stomach hurt and shrunken
She had traveled far
across country
her man's people were
down river

A cool breeze
raised the hair
on her neck,
she then heard the grunt.

It was low, famished
she slowly turned
her eyes,
her neck,
her shoulders,
until she saw It

Its huge arms
hunched over the child
who cried,
It growled again
lifting Its large head

the girl's arm relaxed   near her hatchet
watching the movement of Its eyes
she spoke slowly   with trembling fingers
pulled off her top cover

136

"She's the only one left"

The Bear gazed
watching the girl's mouth
and the movements her eyes
made toward the child,

With one swift movement the bear
turned her powerful body
and ran toward the woods
she watched her go
then turned to feed the child,

    Raven flew over, the sun on his back
    the trees swayed

The woman was not afraid

Thad Poulson

Yvonne Mozée

Yvonne Mozée is an Alaskan-born writer and photographer whose work has appeared in *Alaska Journal, permafrost, Southwest Art, Canadian Ethnic Studies* and elsewhere.

She is a graduate of Nome High School and Willamette University (Piano), and has won awards from the National Federation of Press Women and Alaska Press Women.

Mozée was staff photographer for PACE Magazine (Los Angeles), production secretary on the documentary film "The American Indian Speaks," and editor of The Council for Tanana Chiefs Conference in Fairbanks.

Her maternal grandmother was Athabascan – and she has French, Irish and Scots ancestors as well. She currently lives in Sitka.

Native Bracelet

Tiny beads, forming graceful shapes
      blues, deep red and pink, dense white
      and then clear chartreuse
      to jar, then tickle one's sense of color.

It's a short length of soft hide faced with felt
      enough to go around a wrist
      (a thin wrist, that is – like mine)
      with common snaps sewn on
      sensible, disarming, not very secure.

It's linked so closely to the one who made it
      an Athabascan lady in Fort Yukon
      sometimes in winter the coldest spot in all Alaska
      (of course she could have been part Irish).

She chose the colors, created the design
      the petals and the leaves
      though no doubt she'd seen others
      there in her village where beadwork has been done
      for several – or is it seven now? – generations
      and the women first looked at strange, new pictures
        to copy.

Faint dashes of ballpoint red
      mark her map on the felt background
      linking me to her
      every time I see them.

I suppose her husband or her son killed the moose
      for stew and chops and slippers and dogfood
      or maybe it was a brother
         – sharing is like breathing for them

Yvonne Mozée   139

then the butchering, a wearying tantalizing task
all that future deliciousness
        bloody and near.

Afterward she dealt with the clumsy hide
        scraping and softening
        tough and determined
        already apportioning it for what she wanted to make
        what each one needed.

The beads stitched tightly down
        one by tiny one
        curve together in blossom and stem.

The patience, her tired back, the eyestrain
        sometimes putting her work down to mix some biscuits
        sewing 'til the light was gone
        counting on the dollars it would bring
                for peanut butter
                or gasoline
                or comic books for the grandchildren.

Agpik-Robert Mulluk, Jr.

I am an Inupiaq (Eskimo) from Noorvik, Alaska. I graduated from Mt. Edgecumbe High School in 1969. Afterwards, I joined the United States Marine Corps for four years and got my honorable discharge in 1974 as an E-5 Sargeant. In 1975 I started my college education at Sheldon Jackson College and received my Bachelor's Degree in Elementary Education in 1979. I've been teaching for eleven years at the Northwest Arctic Borough School District. I also am pursuing my Master's degree in administration. My wife's name is Karen and she is an Arikara Indian from North Dakota.

All of the writing I have done so far has usually been for the Alaska Natives. I've shared some of my work in our local newspaper and one state-wide Native newspaper. I know there are many talented writers in Alaska, but they never seem to get the kind of exposure they need to gain some kind of wider recognition. I've found it very frustrating to not be able to show my work and, in fact, I put my "poetry imagination" away for a couple of years.

During this past decade, Alaskan Natives have come of age with their writing. The mode we were in for a long time was by using traditional oral language but if the wisdom of our heritage and cultures is to remain alive, it must also be by writing. Taikuu! (Thank You!)

Proud Iñupiaq

Proud to be born an Iñupiaq,
Nothing to be ashamed of being Iñupiaq.
Because I learn to be an Iñupiaq.
"Real People" they called the Iñupiaqs.
Stories told over and over of the Iñupiaqs.
Strong and healthy our culture was said the Iñupiaqs.
Education we learned but we are still Iñupiaqs.
We act think different but color and skin still Iñupiaqs.
Since birth, to the end, always Proud to be Iñupiaq.

Kobuk Lake Beckons

Kobuk Lake is beckoning me back again.
My blanket of snow is getting thin.
The sun helps daily by getting warmer.
Yesterday I cracked because water flooded my edges.

Soon this beckoning will only get stronger.
I don't know why I do this every spring.
But I know they too want me to leave.
Because I have served my purpose.
Too long of a stay to still be welcomed.

I know when fall's come around.
I will be welcomed again by the real people.
They will cut a hole to put their nets.
The smaller ones will scratch me up daily.
The older ones will blow up my gas bubbles.

Many will walk on me daily to check if I am safe.
Jack Frost is helping me daily.
With his help I will soon be strong enough to hold all.
West and North wind also help once in a while.
Now I am thick enough for Mr. Doo to take his 1st
    run.

The snow flakes is putting my finishing touches.
Again like thousands of years I am repeating my act.
Because the real people need me to survive.
So for eight months I will be till the Kobuk Lake
    Beckons.

Agpik-Robert Mulluk, Jr.   143

Old Village

Few people lived the old style here.
Iñupiaqs you might call them.

They hunted, fished, and trapped for survival.
Each year with no hurry to modernize.

Wood stoves to warm a small log cabin.
Ice was melted to make water.

How quiet and peaceful it once was.
Few to remain at the old village.

All at once a great urgency to move.
But not to down-town but to Noorvik.

If you visit old village now it's very quiet.
The few remnants to show life once lived here.

Our family was the last to live at old village.
How good it was to be a resident of old village.

Eskimo Baby Cries for Me

When the Eskimo Baby cries for me.
My day has come to go.
Yes, he cries for us Eskimo before we leave.

Some dark and lonely night a relative hears him.
He has a name but we don't talk about it.
But we know it dresses in white.

Why? We really don't know.
For animals do know it too.
As you hunt no game is offering itself.

Another sign for me to go.
When my day has come.
Yes, the Eskimo Baby is telling me it's my turn.

The Loneliest Place

As I sat on a bar stool.
I heard a low murmur.
A few talking sensibly.
Hour later talk's getting a little louder.

Two hours later louder yet.
Six hours later a fight starts in the corner.
Soon he no longer murmurs but shouts.
His smoking decreases because he can't light it.

The bar is now a crying place.
Spilling his guts out to total strangers.
Then gets mad and shouts some more.
He soon repeats one sentence remainder of the night.

How lonely a place may be, but it's a regular stop.
Some to have fun but it lasts only a short time.
Many by now don't care if they go work or not.
The loneliest place that got lively for a while.

The next day you woke up with a bad headache.
Too sick to even open your eyes.
You wonder what happened, how did you make it home?
The problem is still within you.

Today you burden your problems with a hangover.
Wishing at times that you weren't so sick.
Wondering how could I quit.
Because you know now you can't find it at the Loneliest Place.

Body, Mind and Spirit of a Strong Iñupiaq

Long ago he used all three
or his existence wouldn't last a day.

Body was kept in shape by Eskimo games.
Mind kept sharp by teasing.

Arguments squared off by footraces.
Points to be made by a story.

Hunting used to feed the body.
Dancing to awaken the spirit.

How strong our people were.
When they used all three.

Now we substitute hard work to develop weak bodies.
T.V. to corrupt the minds to simple thoughts.

Many religions to choose from.
Confusing the spirit of an Eskimo at heart.

Only if we would listen to all three:
body, mind and spirit make strong Iñupiaqs.

Agpik-Robert Mulluk, Jr. 147

Frederick Paul

The following is a chapter of a book to be published in 1990 entitled *Then Fight For It*. This chapter is the story of the conception of the Alaska Native Land claims endeavor. The idea bore fruit on December 18, 1971, when the Congress enacted the Alaska Native Claims Settlement Act. That law is the greatest bloodless redistribution of wealth in the history of mankind. It granted 44 million acres of land and almost one billion dollars to the Alaskan Natives.

Author Frederick Paul is uniquely qualified to tell that story. He is a third generation Tlingit Indian who has fought for the civil rights of the Alaskan Natives.

Tillie Paul Tamaree was his grandmother. She was a member of the Tee-Hit-Ton Tribe (based at Wrangell, Alaska) of the Tlingit Nation. For 65 years she was an employee of the Presbyterian Church, first as a laundress at the Sitka Training School (now the Sheldon Jackson College), then as the girls' advisor, organist, layworker and finally the first female ruling elder of the Church in the synod of Alaska Northwest in 1932.

His father was the first Indian lawyer (in 1920) in the Territory of Alaska and served for two terms as the first Indian legislator (1925 and 1927) in the Territorial Legislature. As the following story indicates, he conceived the idea of Indian property rights through aboriginal use and occupation back in 1925.

Frederick Paul was reared in that atmosphere and, after becoming a lawyer himself in 1940, he devoted his life to the promotion, through the law, of Indian rights. His work culminated in 1966 through 1971 in his representing the Inupiat Eskimos of the North Slope of the Brooks Range of Alaska. That was the situs of the discovery of the largest oil deposit in the North American continent. It was this oil that Frederick Paul asserted was owned by the Eskimos. That thought was considered ridiculous by the oil industry who had already paid the State of Alaska for such rights, by the State who itself asserted ownership, by the Secretary of the Interior who said it was part of the public domain, by the conservationists who wanted to lock it up, by powerful Congressmen who were not about to "give" it to aboriginees and by the Alaska public who were led by businessmen who, in turn, had made application for ownership rights in their personal capacity.

His argument, which so handsomely succeeded, was to arouse the conscience of the United States. We, the Nation, cannot kick off, without redress, the Eskimos from the land they had occupied for thousands of years, land from which they subsisted and which yielded their caribou (some half million), their birds (some millions of them in 147 varieties) and their foxes, brown bears, lynx, wolves, salmon, etc. and, finally, their whales (the sixty footers). They are whalers.

It took him three years to persuade the other competitors that the Natives of Alaska had "legal rights" and if society wanted their land, society should pay fair value. Obviously, it worked.

The following is the germ of the idea conceived and germinated by his father back in 1925 which blossomed in 1971 with the enactment of the Alaska Native Claims Settlement Act.

"Then Fight For It" records the history of the civil rights movement by the Natives of Alaska from the beginning of Russian trade down through the generations to the present day. It will be published by the Howe Brothers of Salt Lake City, Utah in 1990.

One person can make a difference.

The Fox Farmers Drive Off the Indians with Guns: The Origin of the Land Claims Movement©

Icy Strait is one of the fiercest arms of the North Pacific. To the north lies the mainland with its Glacier Bay, Excursion Inlet and Lyun Canal. There must be one hundred glaciers to the north. To the south lies the Alexander Archipelago, commonly called Southeastern Alaska. Icy Strait is the funnel for the northern salmon runs into the inside waters. Many millionaires have been made just from salmon alone out of it, for example, August Buschman sold his Port Althrop fish trap in 1929 for $750,000, only to lose most of it in the 1929 stock market crash.

Hoonah is an ancient Tlingit village nestled in a harbor on its south shore, behind a mountain to protect it from the north wind which whistles down over those one hundred glaciers.

The "Huna" Tlingits were especially hardy, living in that fierce country. And they exercised dominion over it. Two hundred and fifty years ago when Chirikov was exploring there, he put down two long boats full of men just west of Hoonah. They have never been heard from again.

It was there that George Dalton's family for countless generations had been born and reared.

In the spring of 1921, when George was about twenty, his father took the family for their annual garden planting to one of the Inian Islands located in the midst of Icy Strait. For years on this little island they had planted potatoes in the spring to be harvested that fall. Their only fertilizer was seaweed, tons of seaweed, which they would pile on the patch after the harvest. Believe me, they had prime potatoes.

As I say, George had been reared in that country. That island was as much his as the Tee-Hit-Ton country was ours. For centuries his people traversed their hunting trails in that defined area, each family having its hunting cabin, fish camps and berry patches.

When they were bringing their stuff ashore from their gasboat, they heard a shot, a rifle shot, ring out. "Somebody's probably hunting," they surmised.

How mistaken they were. As George stepped out of his skiff, he was met by a man whose name he later learned was Oscar. Oscar was menacing him with a rifle.

"Get the hell out of here," Oscar commanded. "This is my island," Oscar continued. "I got a permit from the Forest Service and the Land Office." They then knew, that shot had been aimed at them!

They left and went back to their winter village, Hoonah. They learned that Oscar had established a fox farm on their island. Raising wild foxes had become very profitable. On small islands, perhaps a mile across, one could turn the foxes loose, for water is a natural fence. All Oscar had to do was to get the strain started and feed them. At harvest time, he could snare them and be on his way to market.

The Daltons were not alone. A couple of dozen others had been ordered off their ancestral lands. They all had a deep anger. By the time the 1924 election took place, the confrontation between them resulted in a plank in the Whiteman's party platform which said:

"Passage of legislation by Congress giving the fox farmers title to lands occupied and improved by them thus ending definitely a possibility that the Indian leaders might succeed in driving ranchers from their island establishments which Paul and his supporters claim belong to the Indians."

For years the annual conventions of the Alaska Native Brotherhood were both serious and festive. All Amy Hallingstad had to do was to stand up and survey her audience. Without a word spoken, the audience caught her humor, the sparkle in her eye. Sam Davis and Sandy

Stevens always had a contest as to who had the biggest, flappiest ears.

The band contest was a highlight, Metlakatla's with Alfred Gordon as their trumpet player, Kake's under the direction of Walter Williams and Ketchikan's with Frank M. Williams as clarinetist. On the last night, there always is a Grand March. What a week.

Sometime during the conventions, Peter Simpson, one of the saints of the Indian movement and long a widower, would keep the delegates and visitors in such suspense until he finally confirmed he was virile enough to take unto himself a bride, that he was still looking and could be caught.

During the 1925 convention, Peter took Dad aside and asked him, "Willie, who owns this land?"

After a long pause, Dad replied, "We do."

"Then fight for it," Peter in a sense commanded, like a laying on of the hands.

Thus was born the Alaska land claims movement.

As I reflect, I think it was the fox farmers who triggered the Indians' determination. It certainly hardened George Dalton's. It was something they could understand, the abrupt ejectment from their garden patches.

The average Indian, as of then, had a fatalism towards the United States. They felt that if the United States decreed it was government land, it was. I can still remember Grampa's saying firmly with conviction, "That's guv'ment land."

It took four years for Dad to convince enough of the Tlingit and Haida leaders to get the Haines 1929 ANB Convention to endorse the idea.

There may be a few people still living today who attended that convention. Frank G. Johnson ("Doc" as we called him because because he had graduated in a premedical course at the University of Oregon) has told and retold the story of that high time. A tribal cousin of mine, Samuel G. Martin, Sr., was the sergeant-at-arms there and today takes pride in his sitting in on the inner council and in his contribution to the Indians' determination. There were many, many others.

The idea then was the United States had already expropriated the Indians' property; thus, the only available method of redress was to sue for its value. The ANB resolution embodied that thought in these words:

"Whereas the United States government has locked up the forest so that what was formerly ours must now be purchased from a government that gave us nothing for it"

The full resolution tells a rather heart-rending tale and here it is:

"Whereas from year to year the condition of the Native Indians of Southeastern Alaska has been getting worse and worse so that they now look toward the future almost without hope; and

"Whereas when the United States government took over Alaska from our forefathers, it was a land of plenty, with rivers teeming with all kinds of salmon, the woods with fur and game animals, and forests were free to use; and

"Whereas the United States Government has locked up the forests so that what was formerly ours must now be purchased from a Government that gave us nothing for it; and

"Whereas our fish streams have been taken from us by the United States Government so that we can neither fish nor live near our ancient fish streams, not only because in the changing civilization the same Government has taught us to live like civilized people and not on a diet of fish like our fathers, but also because our Government without giving us a hearing has prohibited us from catching fish at our ancient fish streams for our support; and

"Whereas the same Government has made fishing regulations so that the only people who can catch fish with profit are those who can afford to invest from ten to twenty-five thousand dollars in a huge fish trap; and

"Whereas all of this had reduced our people till our income averages less than $150 to a family of five all of which endangers the health of our children; and

"Whereas all of this responsibility must be laid at the door of our own Government: Therefore be it

"Resolved, That we petition in the name of The Alaska Native Brotherhood, that great organization of our people comprising over 5,000 Native Indians in Southeastern Alaska, to the Congress of the United States for relief; And it be further

"Resolved, That Congress be asked to delegate a committee of fair minded men to investigate our condition, with money to get the evidence, uninfluenced by the different bureaus which are directly responsible for our condition; And be it further

"Resolved, That copies of this resolution be sent to each Senator and Representative of the Congress of the United States with the hope that some day one may be touched to ask justice for us.

"Adopted by authority of the grand convention of the Alaska Native Brotherhood at their annual convention meeting at Haines Alaska, on November 25, 1929.

> William L. Paul
> Grand President
> Attest: Frank G. Johnson
> Grand Secretary

The Alaska Native Brotherhood hired James Wickersham as its lawyer. Judge Wickersham had been appointed by President McKinley in 1902 as the federal judge to clean up the scandal in the gold fields, particularly at Nome. The incumbent judge, Arthur H. Noyes, had a system whereby one of his cohorts through judicial proceedings got title with the good judge's help to profitable gold claims. Later Judge Wickersham had been delegate to Congress for many years ending in 1920.

He, too, proceeded on the theory that the Indians had already lost their title to the land; he had a fairly good idea, though, of the true nature of aboriginal rights, as we shall see.

When advised of the ANB resolution, Dan Sutherland, as delegate to Congress from Alaska, promptly (in 1930) introduced a bill authorizing the Indians to sue the United States in the Court of Claims for the value of the land they had lost. As a part of our heritage from

England, one cannot sue the government for an injustice without its permission. This theory emanates from the old axiom, "The King can do no wrong," for as the law-maker all the King need do is to change the law defining the wrong so that it would no longer be a wrong.

Sutherland's bill was referred to the Committee on Claims, and there it died. This is a favorite legislative maneuver to kill or give vitality to a bill through assigning it to adverse or friendly committees.

In November, 1930, Judge Wickersham was elected delegate on Sutherland's retirement. He had to give up his employment by the Indians. As delegate, he reintroduced Sutherland's bill and got it assigned to the two committees on Indian Affairs (5 1196, 72nd Congress). Routinely, Congress asks for a report from the executive on proposed legislation. The storm, as in The William Tell Overture, began. It is a storm still blowing today.

The laws of the United States by and large have been good. Through our more than 200 years of life, the United States has formally recognized its trust relationship with its aboriginal peoples. *United States v. Kagama*, decided by the United States Supreme Court in 1886, is fairly representative of the obligations that the United States government has towards Natives. The Court stated:

> "These Indian tribes are the wards of the nation. They are communities dependent on the United States. Dependent largely for their daily food. Dependent for their political rights. They owe no allegiance to the States, and receive from them no protection. Because of the local ill feeling, the people of the States where they are found are often their deadliest enemies. From their very weakness and helplessness, so largely due to the course of dealing of the Federal Government with them and the treaties in which it has been promised, there arises the duty of protection, and with it the power. This has always been recognized by the Executive and by Congress, and by this court, whenever the question has arisen."

The trouble with these good laws is that their execution was entrusted to those who don't pay much attention to them. The theory has been for the Indians to be taught how to adapt to the white man.

Thus in the Alaska situation, back in the early 1930's, the Commissioner of Indian Affairs, G. J. Rhoades, recommended against the enactment of Delegate Wickersham's bill. These are the words:

"After careful consideration of the matter, I perceive no need for the enactment of legislation proposed in §1196."

His exceptions contained in his report related to lands "actually" in their possession for example, the few square feet embraced in a home.

Where the Commissioner got the idea that Alaska was different from continental United States is a puzzle. The Treaty of Cession between Russia and the United States provided

"That the uncivilized tribes will be subject to such laws and regulations as the United States may, from time to time, adopt in regard to aboriginal tribes of that country."

And again in the Act of May 17, 1884, the Congress declared that

"The Indians or other persons in said district shall not be disturbed in the possession of any lands actually in their use or occupation or now claimed by them but the terms under which such person may acquire title to such lands is reserved for future legislation by Congress."

These are good laws, because the genesis of the treaty-making process between the United States and the respective tribes throughout the United States had by this time, 1932, been fully defined. These treaties gave nothing to the Indians; rather, they were a cession by the Indians to the United States reserving to the Indians certain defined areas. That is where the term "reservation" comes from: the Indians "reserving" unto themselves those areas which came to be known as reservations. Thus, in the famous Yakima case of *U.S. v. Winans* back in 1905, the Supreme Court stated:

"In other words, the treaty was not a grant of rights to the Indians, but a grant of rights from them – a reservation of those not granted."

Commissioner Rhoades apparently had never heard of Chief Justice John Marshall's famous words in 1835 that the hunting grounds of the Indians are as much in their actual possession as the cleared fields of the whites, because the Commissioner stated:

"In view of the long, established policy, it seems clear that any actions based upon a general assertion of ownership on the part of the Natives with respect to lands not actually occupied by them would be without foundation of law or fact, and the expense incidental to pursuing this litigation would entail an unnecessary burden upon the Natives not commensurate with any benefits they may hope to secure."

One must remember that Delegate Wickersham's bill simply authorized the opening of the door. In other words, the Commissioner was taking it upon himself to be judge and jury. He held that the Indians had no rights. Since he said so, the door of the courts should not be opened.

The infidelity on the part of the Commissioner of Indian Affairs was, in part, inherent within the Department of the Interior. Thus, the Commissioner reported to the Assistant Secretary of the Interior having charge of public lands. For decades this office of Assistant Secretary was entitled "Assistant Secretary for Public Lands." If the Department of the Interior ruled that the Indians had rights to lands, it would thereby be ruling that the public domain owned by the United States in its proprietary capacity would be lessened. With the emphasis on the part of the Assistant Secretary for Public Lands being placed upon his responsibility to the people of the United States as conservator of the public lands, the Indians always lost that argument. Even with a sympathetic Commissioner of Indian Affairs, the hierarchy of the government was such that the Commissioner was always overruled by the General Land Office, or as we know it today, the Bureau of Land Management.

In this instance, Secretary Ray Lyman Wilbur in his letter of March 11, 1932, wrote:

"After a review of the proposed measure, I agree with the Commissioner (in his report)"

Judge Wickersham had a different idea, as he explained in the hearings:

"But they had a title by occupancy, a possessory title which was of value, and the Supreme Court of the United States had held that that property was of such a value that it could not be forceably taken away from them except by war.

* * *

"Whenever there was an Indian claim of possession, however, it has been the policy of our government from the beginning and the British government prior to that time, to settle with these Natives and procure the quieting of the possessory rights by purchase."

Judge Wickersham told of the genesis of the bill and the part the Alaska Native Brotherhood played as the sponsors of his bill:

"The Alaska Native Brotherhood was organized some years ago, as the best organization that tribes represented in this bill could make of themselves for their own protection. This organization has been in existence now ten or fifteen years. They have a meeting every year. They have an organization, a president and secretary, and they have Southeastern Alaska divided up into districts, have a representative at the head of each district, and they all sign the roll. They meet and have discussions with respect to their rights, and it was at one of these meetings out of which this bill grew. The old men indicated that they ought to have compensation for their lands from the government. They did not know how to get it, but they knew that the Natives in the United States had received it, and they had the matter looked up and discovered that they were in the same category exactly as the Natives in the United States, so they insisted on preparing this bill and making their application to Congress."

The autumn of 1932 brought the Roosevelt landslide. Dad had run as a Republican for Attorney General of Alaska, a territory-wide office. He was soundly defeated, as was Judge Wickersham. It was an ominous time for the Native cause, because Anthony J. Dimond was the Democratic nominee and was elected. Back in 1924 as a territorial legislator, he had sponsored a literacy test for votes, a direct threat to the Indian vote.

But Mr. Dimond was a surprise. As delegate, he saw other Indian tribes throughout the United States petitioning Congress for a redress of their grievances and for authority to bring their claims before the U.S. Court of Claims. He learned that this was not an outlandish idea. He learned that it was simply granting an Indian tribe the right to present their grievances to a court. The idea appealed to his sense of justice.

By the winter of 1934–35, during Dimond's second term in the Congress, he had acquired an immense reputation in the Congress. It was with this political prestige that he brought the proposal of the Alaska Native Brotherhood back to the floor of the Congress.

When Harold L. Ickes was summoned by President-elect Franklin Roosevelt from Chicago to Washington, D.C., he had gone there with the expectation and hope that Mr. Roosevelt would consider him for the job of Commissioner of Indian Affairs. Instead, he became Secretary of the Interior. He was a bright and shining inspiration in that office. Indian affairs remained throughout his career as Secretary a special interest to him.

On March 9, 1935, he wrote Congressman Will Rogers, Chairman of the House Committee on Indian Affairs, endorsing the enactment of the bill authorizing the Tlingits and Haidas to sue the United States. We often call this bill the Jurisdictional Act. A similar report went to the United States Senate.

Dad spent most of the spring of 1935 lobbying the bill through the Congress, being supported by a per diem of $150 per month from the Indian Office. (Mother was teaching and I was at the *Ketchikan Chronicle*).

It was a great day when President Roosevelt signed into law our authority to sue the United States on June 19, 1935.

We all believed that that was a glorious day. The Indians would have monies with which something really fine could be done in this capitalistic world; we could compete in a white man's world with this kind of funding. Certainly it could not have been done without Mr. Dimond's steadfast support and industry.

Gradually, through the years, as we struggled to implement our lawsuit against the United States, I began to realize that the whole concept of pitting Indians against the government and the government against the Indians, aided and abetted by an overzealous Department of Justice, only exacerbated the feeling of frustration, almost akin to a feeling of hatred inside the Indian. Their own government, having stolen their land, was refusing to pay for the same and was fighting tooth and nail never, never to pay them. What kind of social peace does one achieve that way?

George Dalton, Sr., is now in his eighties, one of the venerables of Hoonah and a gentle, gentle man. I knew these stories about the fox farmers, but I had no living witness whom I could name. So, during one of our visits, I asked him, describing briefly the situation. George exploded, "That happened to me. We went to our garden patch and we were ordered off", etc.

Jim Schoppert

Jim Schoppert was born in Juneau, Alaska, in 1947, of a Tlingit mother and German father. Internationally known as a sculptor, with numerous awards and exhibitions, he crafts his poems in much the same way as he crafts his sculpture. Just as he carves the surface of a piece of wood rather quickly with electric tools before doing all the final carving by hand with a crooked knife, his poems come very quickly and are refined over time. The following words of Schoppert's might be as easily applied to his poetry as to his carving:

"My inspiration is drawn from both the Eskimo and Tlingit art traditions. In using the idiom of NW coast art conventions, I've divested it of cultural intent, social meaning, and accustomed appearances, and substituted freedom of color, fragmentation, abstraction, and minimalization. It's from this point I've arrived at these creations which are both modern and speak directly to the continuance and maintenance of the Tlingit cultural identity."

Although he sees himself "as an artist – a visual artist – who occasionally writes," Jim Schoppert's poems have appeared in such publications as *The Greenfield Review*, the *Journal of Alaska Native Art*, and *Turtle Quarterly* and he was chosen as the Outstanding Native American Poet in 1985 in a national competition sponsored by the Native American Center of the Living Arts in Niagara Falls, New York.

Lay the Dark Hills Dreaming

Talkative, excited, compelling
representing something that I had lost
you appeared.

Arriving at that critical juncture
when everything I had created or helped
create
turned ash.

I found myself
crouched
over a long dead fire site
stirring
cold ashes smelling distant meaning and
face pressed rolling
in that ash bed I longed to feel
its warmth.

There was no warmth. There was
no warmth.

Rising Phoenix
your spirit brought the Blue Mountains
into view, uneven horizons rimmed with

purple, magenta, ochre
and in the distance
cloud formations hung geometric
patterns in the sky.

These thoughts are of you.

Thoughts of time we shared float
across my mind
like the vast migration
of Northern Geese we beheld
on our return
from Umatilla.

Ripples upon ripples.

Migrations,
Horizons,
and laughter. I remember well.

And most tender,
a tentative woman,
beyond Blue Mountains where swift
streams flowing
vein the countryside like an old man's
hand.

Beyond the Lavadour hills
beneath the surface of practiced composure
lay
the dark hills
dreaming.

The Effect of Alcohol on Indian People

I fashioned a small airplane
out of yellow paper;
the approximate size and shape
of a milk butterfly.

It floated down
in a long slow spiral
stopping abruptly
as it hit the ground.

Its breeze tilted wings
quivered gently
as if they were petals
of a flower.

I bent to pick it up.

Unlike
a butterfly, however,
it did not rise again
in flight.

The Crying Woman

Here amidst the eddies of Southeast
where Ravens call and
Eagles talon salmon from the channels
I hold a legacy of song and
feel within my heart
the rightful place.

Sweet child
the stars are yours to drape
across your mind in profound wonder
in the manner that the Cedar
laces gracefully this
land of ancient beauty.

O sweet Tlingit child
why do you drink
when all around you
tumbles Cedar?

Prelude to Contact

Our ancient mind
awakens.
A cloud of startled birds

soar to a distant sun
whose rising arc its
zenith had not met

when sails appeared
like clouds
upon a troubled brow.

Between the Rock and the Walrus

Ice beneath my feet
a crushing emptiness above
I stand between
the rock and the Walrus pondering
the conflagration of bridges
left behind. Before me lies
a web of lines criss-crossed
on a mirror.

Stone Carving in Kotzebue

I held the stone
and logic ruled the stroke
of knife
upon that stone.

Shadows
cast by striking light
determined depth of cut
and nuance,
and through it all—

the constant
fingering of the cuts;
the deliberate turning
in my hands to better see
the work progress—

a subtle nature
was revealed.

Glen Simpson

I was born at Atlin, British Columbia in 1941 where my father was working in one of the district's deep placer gold mines. Although my family includes Irish, Scottish, and Kaska ancestry, in the local matrilineal kinship system we are recognized as descendants of Hosentma, a Tahltan woman who was my great-great grandmother.

We lived on the Yukon river near Whitehorse during the Second World War. Although I was a small child, I remember the heavy stern-wheeler traffic on the river and the flights of military aircraft bound for Alaska and the Soviet Union. In 1947 we moved to a remote site on the Alaska highway where, for the next thirty years, my parents operated a roadhouse.

Because of the isolation, I and my brother and sisters, like many children in the north at that time, went away to boarding schools. My brother and I went to high school in Victoria, B.C. – the same school attended by my grandfather fifty years earlier. I went on to the University of Alaska Fairbanks and in 1969 received my MFA from RIT's School for American Craftsmen. I joined the faculty at the

University of Alaska Fairbanks and have taught there for more than twenty years.

Our perceptions are shaped not only by experience and formal schooling but also by our world view. The old Athabaskan beliefs are animistic: everything in the natural world, whether animate or inanimate, has some degree of spiritual power. Within this egalitarian system, people must treat everything with respect. Game animals could choose to avoid an unworthy hunter; fish would by-pass his net. I have even heard of people picking up stones in a prescribed respectful manner.

As a child of the twentieth century I can't claim these old beliefs as my own. There is, however, an influence from them that has come down to me and finds its way into my writing.

Singing Still

An old woman sang
to stop the snow,
voice wavering
through damp canvas
in the soft light of dawn.
She sings to me now
through my father;
still marveling
a lifetime later.

Traveling in the Land of the
Native Art Historians

After a day of viewing the world of Native Art,
sometimes dried and preserved,
I sat in the contrived cozyness of a hotel bar.
How many would puke their cafeteria lunches
if they learned that hunting peoples hunted?
"Raise your hands everyone who knows
the smack of a bullet striking flesh
and has seen the last breath plume
like a small white cloud.
Hold them high please.
Our researcher, in the back of the bar, is counting."

Indians scared some of them;
obvious in that special quick laughter
that surfaces at times like that.
Indians, under the lights,
gave more answers than were their's to give.
But who am I to talk like this;
a man alone with a designer beer,
just an excuse for not going back to that costly room
with its windows permanently sealed against the night air.

Fisheries

He had the badge,
the boots,
the briefcase
full of fuzzy laws.
You need a permit
from the welfare state:
to be Indian,
to fish,
to transport fish,
to be a fish.

Front Street

Front street Nome,
where cultures meet in the mud:
hunters,
whose eyes swept the horizon,
search in a thickening fog,
lost on the drifting ice of an unknown sea
while foraging for one more beer.
Sons of farmers,
seeking what they couldn't find at home,
seek even harder
as they step too heavily
on this last thin edge of America.

Who can tell them
that they are formed in the image of angels?

Stick Dance, Nulato

The urge to silence penetrated every corner,
every child, every rambling drunk.
"Don't look back" said a clear voice,
a woman old enough to tell them of their place;
take only the Spirits of the dead,
is what she really meant.

The door was opened.
Cold fog danced there,
pushing against the breath of men,
reaching out and wrapping each chosen dresser
as they met the night.
All doubt was frozen in that instant
when the Spirits said their last goodby.

She Knew How to Dream

She was a caribou;
dark muzzle dipping
for white moss,
then looking,
looking all around;
head up, nostrils dilating.
Something was different:
somehow, she knew.

The bullet struck
before the sound.
She leapt forward,
faltered,
fell.
The life spilled out of her,
quickly, yet slowly.

She woke up,
still seeing the hunters
walking up from downwind.
She pulled the bag closer;
safe, safe.
Afraid again:
she might have cried out,
frightened others.
Listening,
she could hear only her heart,
pounding strongly,
only her lungs,
drawing in the night air of September.

She knew now
where to go:
upriver, near the hills.
Yes, in the morning
they would break camp.

Grandmother and Raven

"Don't go," they said,
"she wouldn't know you anyway."
They tell me she sits silently
in the shadow at the edge of death;
a leaf that would crackle in your hand.

She smiles now at friends long gone,
walks fields grown to the forests,
puts a shaker in my four year old hand
and tells me I can catch the raven
if only I can salt his tail.

Grandmother, I want you to know,
I'm still trying to catch that raven,
and still looking up to you.

Sherman Sumdum

Hi! My names is Sherman Sumdum. My Tlingit names are Spyune and Shaxoo. I was born in Juneau and raised in Hoonah. I consider myself lucky. I knew my grandparents. Many of my poems relate the stories of how life use to be for the Tlingits. This information came from them. I wrote these poems over an eleven year period. Today I accept that we can never return to the ways of the old, rather we must take the best from the past and incorporate it with the best of today to create a whole new way of life. I hope that you will enjoy these poems and perhaps even find that you too can write of your personal joys and pain so that one day all Alaskan Natives will be strong.

P.S.
Many people have asked me what my name means. For years as a child I thought that it was a name that the Whiteman gave to my forefathers. One day while my wife was working on our family tree she located the name SUMDUM: the booming sound of the ice as it is breaking from the glacier. Many have said that my voice does boom. Hopefully my poetry will boom across the state so that others will not have to learn the hard way.

I am Chookaneidi' and proudly carry the Eagle tradition of my mother's people originally from Glacier Bay.

The Russians Came

Arriving like Raven
Seeking the water's "gold"
Taking, seldom giving
Russians came.
Killing and enslaving
Leaving Creole young
Bringing diseases
Starvation, pain
Selling what wasn't theirs
Departing like locust
Devastation
Heartache
Still remain!!

Why?

GRANDFATHER you watch from above
This was your father's land
Now I am forbidden
From walking in your way
You said this would be mine
Washington says no!
My skin still glows brown
Under the same sun
Which once warmed your soul
Washington says I must be "white"
GRANDFATHER your way
Survived centuries
You gave to the poor
You respected the elders
You shared your experiences with young
You fed and clothed your family
You never stole
You lived in peace
You never took more than you needed from Mother Earth
You laughed, sang and cried
You truly were a man
The great book the preacher carried
Spoke of all the things you did
Regardless of name given
You lived according to their God
Never knowing a book was necessary
To instruct in living the proper way
You lived as one with mankind, animals and the land
I fail to understand
You promised me this land
Washington says no!
WHY?

Days of Old
Days of New

drums BEATING
HUMMING voices
DANCING shadows
night owl's CRY
waves SLAPPING
food SHARED
elder RISES
story TOLD
babies WHIMPER
mothers COO
lullabye SANG
PEACE EXISTED!!

gavel BANGING
anger INCREASING
sides TAKEN
votes COUNTED
hills BARREN
timber GONE
fish racks EMPTY
t.v. BLARING
children ABUSED
boundaries DRAWN
DISHARMONY EXISTING!!!

Native Corporation

TLINGIT
belonging to the land.
Free to wander anywhere
Signing pieces of paper
Who was my father's father?
Village
Regional   CORPORATIONS
Not the land
But government
Stocks replace fish drying
Dividends replace hides curing
Corporate meetings replace tribal houses
Voting replaces storytelling
We are of the land
                    not governments
This has been forced upon us
Choices were never ours
Our forefathers taught us well

WE WILL SURVIVE
WE WILL ADAPT
WE WILL SUCCEED
WE WILL THRIVE

WE WILL BEAT THEM AT THEIR OWN GAME!!

Compromise

WE HAVE MADE SO MANY COMPROMISES
TRADING

bow and arrows	for	guns
kayaks	for	motorized boats
dog sleds	for	snow machines
native speech	for	english
subsistence	for	food stamps
independence	for	dependence
seal skin parkas	for	down coats
tundra	for	cement
stars	for	street lights
moose meat	for	hamburger
wholeness	for	fragmentation

THE TIME HAS COME . . .
DO WE FADE AWAY OR MAKE OUR VOICES HEARD
COMPROMISE OR UNITE?

We Are the Land!

Native people are a curiosity?
Viewed with pity,
Ignored age old cultures.
Refusing assimilation
Choosing not only to survive
But to THRIVE.
Pipelines built
Rivers damned
Ancient hunting grounds
Changed, no more.
U.S. Government
State bureaucrats
Turn deaf ears
On pleas
Providing token land
Cash in hand
Neither which we've seen.
Sovereignty
Subsistence
Common identities
Cannot be taken away
They exist in our hearts.
Religion replaces spirituality.
Languages lost or changed
Technology arrives
These cannot destroy
Our oneness with the land.
Our desires
Our dreams
Strike fear
We will vanish they predict
Justice will prevail

Not because of man's law
Not because of corporate stock
Not because of business success
We will survive
We will unite
We are the land
Therefore we will live on!

*Written after reading the EPILOGUE by Judge
Thomas R. Berger in "VILLAGE JOURNEY."*

Bring Pride to Our Land

It would be so easy
                    To turn the other cheek
We have so many times.
Pressures of the world
Close in around us

    But is that our choice?

        Have we become so obsessed with
        two spirits?

Have we forgotten
From whom we came
GRANDFATHER fought the land
Claiming it daily for his own
Now we relinquish it
Without taking a stand
Dig deep within your heart
Find the strength our people once had
To fight the elements . . .
              TO SURVIVE
It is there awaiting rebirth
Allow it to come forth
End the day
Knowing you are
        a MAN
          a WOMAN
            a CHILD

Who brought PRIDE to our land!!!

Mary TallMountain

GOING THROUGH CHANGES might be the title of my life's story. Having sprung from a hugger-mugger meld of ancestors, I find I am unbelievably various and interesting, even to my self. I see my self a tot beside the mystical Yukon River, she who centered my mindset early, who colored the lives of all my Indian forebears, that river remote, stately, mischievous, illogical, and rowdy, whose beauty coils unforgettable in the seedbed of my mind.

Violent revolt ensued when I was taken from my beloved village, Nulato, and from my mother and brother. The adoptive parents returned with me to Alaska. I continued explosively through my teens and a botched young marriage. I mutinied, sometimes in dignity, sometimes with raunchy curses. From each level in this alien culture, I reaped something to put into my bag of laughs and tears.

"Changeable, she is," they said (the immutable They who stand in judgment at the edges of our lives). Yes! change was and is the essence of my nomadic people. I've never lived in one place or stayed on one job longer than two years. The unknown over the next hill captivated me. Changes slowly altered me. I observed closely and learned from everything I could see or otherwise sense. When the time came, I slipped as comfortably into my niche as a hand into a silk glove, realizing it as my vocation, my obligation, to observe and to write of any alienated people I encountered, chiefly of the Alaskan Natives.

Daily, strength comes from the Source. It is wonderful to have passed through the main changes and emerged mellow and wiser, able to pass some wisdom on to other women younger or elder, to help them write for themselves happy and creative aspects.

Outflight

Galena Air Service's little Red Baron bounces and dawdles along, the pilot intent on where to thrust through a fluff of cirrus clouds. Why don't we fly around the enormous cloud bank? No, we skim through the towering top. Drafts jerk us up, down, and around. Here in the body of the cloud, the Arctic chill says we're in Alaska. The other four passengers, and I, and the pilot, shiver in our down jackets but it's not long before the bushplane is buzzing out into the blue.

Jagged peaks needle up like shards of brown glass. Beyond, we crane at endless fragments of another cloud as we float before Denali, that breathtaking mountain renamed McKinley a long time ago. Today her snow cap lies under veils; her sorrel-colored attendants, Brooks, Hunter, Foraker, Russell, a grandeur arrayed below her. Beneath their snowlines countless blackish-green spruce trees stream down the slopes. Scientists call these four mountains massifs, and they *are* massive. They compose most of the Alaska Range. We will cross the less formidable Kuskokwim Mountains and the yet smaller Kaiyuh Mountains, before we arrive at our destination, the subarctic bush.

I'm busy reliving another autumn day in 1978, when I had flown this route over the inconceivably vast Interior on my way to my birthplace. That was the day I had returned for the first time to my roots in the Yukon village of Nulato, after an absence of fifty years. We had found fewer clouds than these, and a more intense clarity of the air. The mountains had lain breathing the light, and the valley had stretched to the horizons, the autumn gold and bronze of its surface formed a rough pitted pumpkin pie magnified to the *nth* power.

That afternoon in Anchorage I had boarded a six-passenger Nomad out to the River. In the seat ahead, a tall slim half-blood Native woman was reading. She called to her daughter, Minnie, a chubby child about five, who was tossing and catching a pair of purple beaded earrings while chattering indiscriminately to the pilot, her mother, her puppy, and two snoring young Indian men. She wore scrubbed cord coveralls and a sunflower yellow sweatshirt. Her hair was a sooty horsetail, eyes gleaming blackberries. Crawling across my lap to look out the narrow windows of the plane, she was the epitome of knees and elbows and energy. She was delightfully huggable, I learned during one of her lap-crossings.

The two young Indians had no problems sleeping, but Minnie's puppy couldn't even doze. She set up a tiny dirge. Bushplanes aren't always well insulated; winds bellow and engines roar; and sometimes the plane does a jig in sudden, unexpected drafts. Minnie made faces and clapped her palms over her ears, but it didn't help, so she consoled the puppy with a wrassling match. This pup wasn't your real Alaska malemute, but she was the most cunning pup I'd ever met. She was the color of a birch leaf in fall. A pale champagne-colored X lay across her shoulders, long flirty eyelashes the same color batted back and forth, and her ears drooped like empty silk gloves. Minnie called her Sheba. When I told Minnie how pretty Sheba was, my admiration encouraged Minnie's mother to introduce herself as Vernita. She had come in on Alaska Air from a visit to Seattle; our bush pilot was Garth; and the two snoozing young Indians had been on R&R in Anchorage. I learned further that the salmon runs were about over; it had been a real good year for dog salmon and not so good for King. Blueberries, Vernita said, were falling off the bushes; she had put three gallons in the freezer. Her husband had told her on the phone he had shot his first moose of the season, and Vernita sighed with a certain pride, saying her hands would be full for a week skinning out, cutting up, freezing, and cooking that big moose. She thought it would be an early winter this year. Something had told her, in the way the balsam leaves were turning.

Garth remarked, "We're a hundred miles south of the Arctic Circle," undoubtedly wanting to enlighten me, the newcomer the Natives called "Cheechacko." We crossed the pale violet Kaiyuh Mountains, site of our people's hunting grounds, I was informed, long kept a deep religious secret from other bands of Indians along the River. The Yukon was visible now, a silver corkscrew lying in the folds of the enormous marsh country. Already the air was darkened by flocks of geese, flurrying and rising to take the southbound Pacific Flyway, high above us and to the east. I felt the plane merely inched along in the immensity of space as we crossed the last lap of the central plain, but Garth remarked that the light played tricks. Ahead, the Yukon unfurled in a coil of river and creeks like ribbons of fallen sky. Garth showed me some islands the River had created by dropping silt in a huge flood a few years back. He pointed down to the curve of a marsh. "See the moose?" he asked.

I said, "I can't see it at all, it's just a dot!"

Vernita chuckled, but Garth got me off the hook, "He's just a dot from here. Down there, he's bigger than a piano."

Then I had rested back in my seat. It had been my first bushplane trip, and after four hours I was tired. Minnie and Sheba had curled up in her seat and were asleep. Looking at them, I thought I had been only as small as Minnie when I had left Alaska. How little I had known then, how little I had learned since, about this strange country of my birth. For a moment I regretted the years lost, but lulled by the vast river and sky, I felt safe and slept.

Now, an air pocket jolts into my half-dream. This isn't the Nomad! But what plane is it? Where are Minnie and Sheba? Why, of course, I realize, I've been dreaming about my first flight to the Yukon, seven years ago. This is 1985, and I'm in the Red Baron, and it's hovering. We're getting ready to sit down at Nulato; I can see the shining galvanized iron roofs of the village. The pilot's apparently new to this run; with minute care he's studying wind drafts, always tricky here around the great upjutting bulk of Cemetery Hill. There! He's got it. He swings the Baron sharply out over the River and back in a grand wheel, and we dip slow over the hill. It is capped with clusters of white-painted picket fences, sheltering the graves of one of the famous Alaskan cemeteries. The pickets gleam like white baubles in the afternoon sun, slanting above the silty red-grey River. We hiccup to a stop on the gravelly tarmac.

There's Cousin Andrew, outside. I see he has children with him. Maybe they are some of the young Koyukon Athabascans I've come to read my poetry for. Now I feel that I'm really home. The pilot jumps out, and for an instant we passengers crowd together in the narrow aisle. Then we step down into a babble of welcoming voices against the sudden quiet of the gold aspens bending like sentinels towards us.

Gaal Comes Upriver

Deep in the Bering Sea
Gaal flicks her heavy tail.
Majestic with her mates,
Enters the Yukon tides
Swimming north
To the place of Midnight Sun.

Steady in the brown river
She cleaves the miles.
Her fearless eyes
Know swoop and nip of gulls,
Menace of rolling logs,
Black waiting shapes of Bear.

Driven traveler
With one compelling course,
She will not feed again
On the ancient pilgrimage
To the tiny creek of spawning
Only her genes remember.

In the immense ponder of noon
She rests with the others,
Crimson shadows lying still
Beneath a sheltered bank
Far from
Icy sea, their home.

---

*Gaal is the Athabascan Indian word for King Salmon, who start the
spawning flight from Bering Sea to the Yukon River in early May.

Out they stream.
Hidden nets rise to catch.
Gaał flashes wild,
Rosy silver, she arrows
Above hunched backs,
Falls into the circle.

The net tautens.
She hangs to it, thrashes,
Shoots to the surface,
Arches, lunges, flutters
Away from the churning mass,
Above dismay and gaping jaws.

Gaał jackknifes free,
Sweeps on upriver.

An Old Athabascan Complaint
Entitled
Gisakk Come, He Go

We here long time.
We live on salmon, bear.
We care for land.
    Gisakk come, he go.

He freeze self. Lose dogs.
He burn lungs. Lose legs.
He waste everything. Meat, fish.
    Gisakk come, he go.

Mosquito bite him.
He wear wrong clothes.
He drink, lose trail.
    Gisakk come, he go.

He don't talk right, don't
Know when to sit down, get up.
He make too much talk talk.
    Gisakk come, he go.

He spend too much *dinga*.
He gamble away his house.
He lose his wife.
    Sometime Gisakk go.
    Maybe he go for good.

Among native Alaskans, their word for Anglos is *Gisakk*; early Russians talked a lot about Cossacks, and the new word was born.

A Quick Brush of Wings

Olivia tells:
One time just before breakup
K'ilmoya, little Beaver
In Mukluk Slough, stick up her head.
Look around, say: How are you?
Kids run home scared.
We go down, she's gone.

Last winter, Tatiana says,
Albert's getting water.
He yell, *Yoona-oo! Yoona-oo!*
There's Christmas tree, sure enough,
Shining on Yukon river ice.
It's like a bush on fire.
In the morning it's gone.

Lidwynne nods. Same night,
My dog Grumpy start howling
In woman's voice. I go out.
She's staring like Owl at nothing.
I don't know what it is.
A few days later
That poor Grumpy go crazy!

Marie snips a tail of sinew.
When Nicky is in hospital down Tanana
I'm on death watch.
Cold fingers touch my neck.
Feel just like icicle dripping.
I hear feet walk away.
Right then the old man die.

Something cold feathers my arms —
A quick brush of wings. I tell them
Across an ocean I had dreamed
Dotson, the Raven, flying
Upside down.
His eyes were like red coals.

Ahhh! The sewing women
Suck in their breaths.
Lots of spirits all over, this year,
They whisper.

The Light on the Tent Wall

For Mary Joe, my mother

There was a light. Suffused
onto the canvas through mother's womb.
Her round belly turned the
tent wall pink. There was humming,
Soft talk about the baby coming.
Women, mothers, warm by the
Yukon stove, visiting Mary Joe
and her child, I who lay unborn
in her cradle of light.

Years came. I was taken
where there were no tent walls,
where I had to dream my own,
and as time passed, often
I saw the light on the wall,
no longer pink, it was
Fire, its tongues licking
the tent wall.
Fire of our life, flickering.

Light returned where I was,
moving through far places, years.
Not suffused now. Gone
the voices, singing. Useless,
wind plucked with
chill fingers at the wall.
Often the sound was angry,
hasty, wanted to speak
But could not find words.

1987

I overtook it, brought back
my dream. Light dyed the canvas
the color of mother's blood
gliding through her womb,
through labored lungs,
through death, and I
remembered the color of her blood,
light on the tent wall,
painted by my infant dreams.

Sometimes I still hear
Angry winds plucking mutely
At the wall. The light is there too,
and thinking of the watching women
I wonder whether they
saw the light on the tent wall.
I saw it plain before my birth
and held it a half century.
I will hold it forever.

Brother Wolverine

girl child
they took you so far away
upriver I hear
the mailboat whistle
my heart jumps
waiting for words from you

snaa',
I miss you
when the children shout
down by the slough and
when I see leaves of *k'eey*
dance in the white wind

in pictures you sent
you wear the fawnskin parka
I sewed with little sinew stitches
by the light of our coal-oil lamp
around your face I see
the gray ruff of Wolverine

he has *yega* of power
his ruff can stop
the winter winds
from freezing your breath
into needles of ice —
I give you his fur

---

snaa' = little child
k'eey = birch tree
yega = spirit

Wolverine, we call *Doyon*
the Chief,
snarled in my trap —
bared his teeth, bit the air
it was his last battle
he came home with me

Brother Wolverine
let your fur warm my girl child
guard her in far strange places
make her fearless like you
do not let her forget us
Brother Wolverine

Grandmother's Dream

Grandmother!
I see you sleeping.

Is your *tlamass* flashing
Through silver scales of *Gaaɫ*?
Your brown old hands are trembling.

Does *K'olk'eeya*, the Hawk,
Struggle in your snare?
Your tired arms are waving.

Is your shiny hair blowing
Black in the wind above your net?
Your gray head is quiet.

Are you dancing like *hodaalk'un*
Who burns the forest birches?
Your little moccasins shuffle.

Is that Grandfather, young again,
Impatient at your tent?
Like a wild rose by the river,
Your wrinkled face is smiling.

Grandmother!
I see you sleeping.

1977.

The Figure in Clay

Climbing the hill
When it was time,
Among sunken gravehouses
I filled my fists with earth
And coming down took river water,
Blended it,
Shaped you, a girl of clay
Crouched in my palms,
Mute asking
To be made complete.

Long afterward
I buried you deep among
Painted masks.
Yet you ride my plasma
Like a platelet,
Eldest kinswoman.
You cry to me through smoke
Of tribal fires.
I echo the primal voice,
The drumming blood.

Through decades waiting
Your small shape remained.
In morning ritual
You danced through my brain,
Clear and familiar.
Telling of dim glacial time,
Long perilous water-crossings,

For my Grandmother, Matmiya, an Athabascan woman.

Wolf beasts
Howling the polar night,
Snow flowers changing.

Now, watching you in lamplight,
I see scarlet berries
Ripened, your
Sunburned fingers plucking them.
With hesitant words,
With silence,
From inmost space
I call you
Out of the clay.

It is time at last,
This dawn.
Stir. Wake. Rise.
Glide gentle between my bones,
Grasp my heart. Now
Walk beside me. Feel
How these winds move, the way
These mornings breathe.
Let me see you new
In this light.

You —
Wrapped in brown,
Myself repeated
Out of dark and different time.

1981.

The Women In Old Parkas

snapping gunshot cold
blue   stubborn lips clapped shut
the women in old parkas
loosen snares   intent and slow

they handle muskrat   Yukon way
appease his spirit *yega*
bare purple hands
stiffen   must set lines again

*   *   *

night drops quick black
in winterhouse   round shadows
cook fresh meat soup steam floats
skinny bellies grumble

they pick up skinwork   squint
turn lamp-wick down kerosene
almost gone   sew anyway

oh! this winter is the worst
everything running out not
            much furs
they make soft woman hum . . .

but hey! how about those new parkas
we hung up for Stick Dance!
how the people sing!
how crazy shadows dip and stomp
on dancehouse walls! their
remembering arms rise like
                  birdwings

* * *

at morning they look into the sky
laugh at little lines of rain
finger their old parkas
think: spring is coming soon

1981

Lincoln Tritt

My name is Lincoln Tritt, I was born in Salmon River (now abandoned) Alaska, 1946.

My childhood years were spent moving back and forth yearly between Ft. Yukon and Arctic Village (now considered home). The first twelve years of my life were spent in rural Alaska with a lot of traditional experience along with traditional native teaching. This kind of teaching has really helped a lot in later life when decisions had to be made.

Around the age of thirteen I was sent to a boarding school. From this time my education was in the modern system except for summer vacations which were spent at home. Here, I've tried to get as much understanding of the modern technology. As a result, I have held many jobs from construction to teaching, along with my hobbies of photography, music and space science.

But my greatest education came from my study of my native people. I have never accepted the idea that one system has all the answers. My studies have proved me right.

It is my opinion that if anybody wants a thorough education, they should learn more than one society. This is not only an important education, it will also open their eyes to a lot of things they only fantasize about.

Memory of My First Year

Some of my first memories or visions of my early days come in tiny pieces. I think the first one is of crossing a wide creek, either in late winter or early spring. I always thought it's the one right next to Fort Yukon, they called TR'AANJIK. I was in a toboggan with my father at the handle. Possibly my mother and brother were in the toboggan with me. I've always thought of our dogteam looking like the ones that are on the cover of the Alaskan Churchman news magazine, the one that the Episcopal Church in Alaska publishes. I think we were getting into Ft. Yukon, because of the jubilation I sensed around me. After all Salmon River Village was quite a long ways and according to an article I read in the *Daily-News Miner* by a lady name of (Mike) Dalton, it was supposed to have been a winter of record cold. Anyway, if my research into timetable is correct I would have been no more than four months old.

I also remember being in a toboggan on a lake, but I figured it must have been later, because it seemed to be a different time of the season – there was no ice along the shore of the lake in front of a hill. So it must have been spring and that was the extent of that vision. My mother tells me we were in the Christian Village area then. So as it turned out, it wasn't later but just before the instance mentioned above.

This next memory was confirmed by my mother, because I remember her sitting there. When I asked her in later years, she told me I was about one year old. I remember sitting in a jump-up thing, I never knew the name of it. But I think I heard someone call it a Johnny Jump-up. Anyway it had these big wooden beads on it, about half-inch in diameter and about three on each side. I think one was red, another green. I don't remember the last one. What I remember about it was the taste. I remember bending down to taste it and I didn't like the taste at all. Kinda made me sick, a little. From that moment on, I never again had any interest in those kind of objects. This was in Arctic Village. So that means I'd already traveled to three places by the time I was one.

From here my memories or visions have more contents or details, so they must've happened when I was a little older. But I was still the baby, because I have no memory of a baby brother then.

I remember that we were living on a side of an almost flat hill by a lake. According to my mom this was a river, most likely the Salmon River. There might have been a lake on the other side. There was still ice on the river, but the ground was devoid of snow as far as I could see, although my vision probably only extended to where I was carried. It might have been spring, if there was snow on the ice. A plane came in that day. Something like a Piper Cub. I think I was too young to meet the plane. There is always a conflicting thought in this, in that my memory goes back and forth between a cabin and a tent. I think somewhere along the way I was playing with this memory and got it confused. Anyway, my dad and brother came back from the plane with a package. There might have been more but what I remember is a cowboy outfit for my older brother. I really thought it was something, because I think I'd heard of Gene Autry at that point in life. Anyway it wasn't strange at all, but very familiar. My parents must've talked about it or I must have seen something like it somewhere. Although some of my visions only came back to me years later, this one has always stayed with me. My mother also told me later that this was the Salmon River Village and it was a small cabin.

Another vision I have before most of my memories became more detailed is of me, my brother and mom at a camp with my grandma, uncle and aunt. There might have been more people, but it's pretty sketchy. I seem to remember it because of a story of that place. The place is called TSEEGWAAJYAA VAVAN. There is a tale of a person's skull on the shore. If you throw the skull into the water, you will find it on the shore again. There is a story behind this but I don't remember it. Anyway I remember I wasn't able to go to the lake, but my brother, uncle and aunt played there and I think they talked about it, when they came back. As I said, for some reason this thought is very sketchy to the point that it might have been a dream. But I have an idea of the land. I couldn't see the lake, but there were trees and patches of brushes around our tents. This, too, was later confirmed by my mom and I was pretty accurate.

Just to dispel some of my doubts, I discussed these stories with my mom and she confirmed all of them. The sequence, I guess, was not in order though, because according to her and some records I have seen. I was born in Salmon River and from there we went to Ft. Yukon by way of Christian Village by dog team and then up to Arctic Village. All this was within the first year of my life.

There was another experience I remember, but I can't place the point in time. I suppose I was a little older because for one thing we were kinda settled for the time being and also I could stand so I must've been able to walk. I went with my father to either check a fishnet or put one in. Anyway, this instance always reminds me of the gingerbreadman story. I remember when we were leaving the village, Grandma Mary was baking. I think it was bread or something. It had to raise and this along with hearing the gingerbreadman story at the same time must be the reason that they relate to me. Or perhaps it was just the word "bread" in each. I can still imagine a gingerbreadman running up the river trail. This was also my first experience with red fish. We went to Redfish Lake and caught a few.

These memories lead me to assume that a good percentage of my childhood was spent outside or in the woods and not too much inside. I can still remember how the inside of a fur (caribou) parka smelled when I put it on.

A Glimpse of the
Aboriginal Society

Imagine a land bare of people and anything made by man. Which would leave us with rocks, plants and animals.

Now imagine man in that environment, sans clothing, shelter or tools of any kind, because all these were made by man.

This is, in essence, the very beginning of man. All he has at this point is his survival instinct and faith.

Since he was not equipped with the physical abilities of other animals. He must use what he has, mainly his brain and his ability to reason. With these, he fashioned tools, which substituted for his lack of strength, speed and agility.

At this point in time his only purpose is to survive. Most of his time is spent hunting and gathering food, because his tools are pretty crude and primitive. As his tools and hunting ability improves, he starts to have some time in which to think of better and easier ways to survive.

It is natural to protect your offsprings, so in order for man to make life a little easier for his children he starts telling his children stories. A lot of the stories are from this man's own experience and thoughts since he does not want his children to make mistakes that he has already made and learned from. Parts of these teachings become skills and the parts that involve living with others become moral and personal values. This is very important since an individual cannot survive alone, since they lack the physical abilities that animal has. One person cannot get enough food to last. Small animals, no matter how many, cannot satisfy all of man's requirement. Larger game is required — which also requires more than one man or better tools. It requires tribal effort.

According to legends, our story's location is at the

source of the Porcupine River – at least that is where our legendary hero CH'ITEEHAAKWAII presumably starts.

Our people, the NEETS'AII or NEETS'IGWITCH'IN, being a nomadic tribe, were not always restricted to this valley. Some elders believe that our kinship extends throughout interior Alaska, that some of our relatives are still living in Bettles, Stevens Village, and other places in Alaska and Canada.

The caribou fences in this area were used probably in the 1700's and early 1800's. They were used only in the fall and the rest of the year was spent following the herd. The migrating paths of the herd extends up to the coast and over into Canada and back. The caribou migration habits were unaltered from earlier times. Even as late as the 1950's or 60's they were expected up on the east ridge on July 15th and on the west ridge on Sept. 22nd. To my best recollection, they always showed up. According to the way the caribou fences are set up in this area, these migration habits can be verified. As a result, the lives of our people were fairly simple, since their means of hunting and fishing were very limited. They did not have much choice in their way of life. In order to survive they had to follow the herd. This, in turn, strengthened their faith, since their faith in their knowledge of the caribou habits was all they had to depend on.

Their means of hunting were very limited. They could only get so much range and power from their bow and arrows. As a result they had to be strongly dependent on each other. The caribou, at the time, were very sensitive and would take off at the slightest sound, sight or smell. This forced the people to work together. The more the people worked together, the more they got to know each other, which was the basis for their social structure. In order for them to acquire a caribou, it had to be herded to within killing range of their weapon or into their snares.

How a person was judged depended on his ability to make the best tools and weapons and his ability to acquire food. Some called them "Lucky (in obtaining food)." Generally these people were "richer" in the sense that they could provide for more people. It was usually these people who were in charge of hunting and distribution of food. They also took in widows and orphans at times, which today is defined as polygyny.

Again as I have stated earlier, people forced to live together get to know each other very well, so law and order understood without being written down. Since the distribution of people throughout this country was pretty sparse, they did not mix very often. Also this is where the elders fit into the society. Since they had lived longer and experienced more, they were more knowledgable in behavior and experience. Their wisdom was very important to the society. As a result most of the young boys and girls were taught by their grandparents or uncle or aunts. Respect for older persons was taught from the beginning of comprehension, since that is where all their learning was going to be coming from.

The knowledge also put the elders in the position of judges. When a person was to be banned from the tribe, which is an ultimate punishment for an ultimate crime, it was usually decided by the elders. Most other misdemeanors were punished by being ignored by everyone for a time.

Since life was the teacher in most cases the older a person was, the more respected he or she was.

Any knowledge outside of life, which today would be defined as scientific, was usually left to the shaman. This did not only include medicine but also parapsychology and other scientific knowledge and ability. This knowledge gave the shaman his power, which he kept secured, since too many people with power often led to conflicts.

This is also the political structure that was derived from their nomadic existence.

One major difference between our people and that of the dominant society today is humility. Among our people, no matter how far or how high a person goes, they know they are small in the presence of God and universe.

Prior to contact, it would be very hard to know if people actually lived on this land. People, as a rule, did not leave traces of themselves anywhere. Even killing sites were cleansed after game had been butchered.

Children were taught to be quiet at infancy, since most of life involved hunting.

Unlike modern society which, in most cases, is based on materialistic value, earlier society required more personal and moral values.

Haven

Sometimes the atmosphere of the moment can move you to do something totally unexpected.

When I was about four years old, I remember waking up in the middle of the night. The kerosene lamp was turned up and the stove was blazing hot, so I knew my father was up as he usually was. I remember he got up about five in the morning, I suppose to heat the house before he went back to bed.

The house felt so comfortable and the quiet gave you a sense of peace that was very hard to imagine during the day. Our beds were against the back wall and the stove sat in the middle of the house. He was sitting on the other side of the stove with his back to the stove sipping a cup of tea.

The peace overwhelmed me so much that I had to get up and enjoy a piece of it. So I got up and put on my clothes. At the time our clothes were made of caribou fur so getting dressed was simple. Surprisingly there was no comment from my dad as I made my way out the door.

The night was very quiet and clear. At that time electricity was non-existent in the village so there was nothing to break the silence or the darkness. If it was cold, I wasn't aware of it.

Our door was on the side of the house and it was dark there so I went to the front where the light from the house cast a glow on the snow. Since there was no one to play with I spent the time rolling around on the snow and then laid back and wondered about the stars. I wanted to stay longer but, eventually the thought of a character in one of our horror stories began to haunt me so I had to go in.

My dad was still sitting there as I took my clothes off and got back into bed. I just knew my sleep was going to be peaceful and very pleasant.

Whatever happened to me later in life, no matter how unpleasant, I always knew I had this little sanctuary in the whole of the Universe.

Lincoln Tritt   217

Winton Weyapuk Jr.

My parents live in Wales, Alaska, a small village 50 miles from the
Siberian coast. They've seen many changes in their life, including the
changes I've made in my own life. I am living for now in Fairbanks
but very often in my mind I spent part of the day there in Wales. The
village lies at the base and hillside of a beautiful mountains. Many of
our ancestors lie there among the boulders. When my mind is troubled I draw strength and peace from thoughts of that mountain and
the people living there in Wales.

Fairway Rock, 1981

"when my heart is overwhelmed:
lead me to the rock
that is higher than I."
Psalms 61:2

Weatherbound for two days,
we watched birds, picked wild cabbage,

sat on rocks in the lee of the island and
turned cold, brown faces to the sun.

Our boat was pulled up at the only
place possible,

A large flat boulder,
  used by generations of

hunters and hunted
seals, walrus, birds, men.

We watched in amazement as
  a seal surfaced

in front of an iceberg
  overturning.

On Cape Mountian

Bones of my ancestors
Lie among boulders on
The hillside. Alone
But for the company

Of their world possessions,
Preserved by ice, cold winds,
Warnings to respect the dead.

The chemicals of life
Leach down, and a
Saxifrage springs up
From where a hand once lay.

The Land Cares for its Own

In memoriam: L. L. Natungok

For two weeks the land kept its
secret shrouded in ice-fog and snow.
Search parties returned each day
having gone a few miles into the
whiteness that was earth and sky.

Finally, darkness revealed stars.
The searchers prepared for an
early start. Twenty miles from
home they found the tracks of
his snowmobile moving in a
straight line over steep hills
as if guided by a faulty compass.

His campsite was found the next
day, snowmobile in a creek, tarp
spread over willows, sled, and
campstove – dry matches placed
beside it.

His footprints led towards a
shelter cabin twelve miles away.
A plane circled and dipped, the
searchers converged.

From a distance he looked like a
tussock, hair waving gently, like
dry grass in the wind. He lay,
snowsuit unzipped, mittens and
hat cast aside, as if he died
feeling too warm.

Winton Weyapuk, Jr. 221

Wooden Pots and Heated Stones

Her eyes belie
  her aged face, her
memory as quick as
  her movements are slow.

"I was one of
the paddlers," she says,
  her fists describing
an arc. When we

reached the small island
we cooked a meal in
wooden pots filled with
water, dropping heated
stones into them.

When the water began to
boil, we ladled out the
stones and replaced
them with meat.

That was how we did it
long ago," she says,
gazing out at the
small island, her hands
clasped at her lap.

The Dancer

*"How shall we proceed
in the right way?"*

Kingikmiut dance song

As he begins
  he keeps his hands
directed inwards
  contains the power of
the song. Gloves protect

        the spirits from human
        corruption, or do they

protect him? He draws
  energy from the audience.
His
  neck
is
  as
fluid

        as a loon's, dancing
        on a lake. Body follows
          head, eyes
              follow hands.
        Stamping feet bounce him
        an inch off the floor.

Drummers, singers and
  dancer—in perfect
harmony—perform
  once for the good spirit,
once for the bad.

Winton Weyapuk, Jr. 223

Seal

Whose thirst forms
   the cycle
   rises in the breathing hole.

The hunter waits,
   one breath, two
   stopping his own to convince

seal there is
   no one. Then
   his harpoon explodes through snow

cover, severs
   neck bones, lodges
   secure under skin.

The hunter pulls up seal,
   makes snow water
   in his mouth

then squirts it in
   seal's mouth to
   release its slaked spirit.

ACKNOWLEDGEMENTS

All the work in this anthology is printed with the consent of the original authors. Copyright remains in their names and reprint permissions should be requested of the authors. Special thanks are extended to the following publications where these works first appeared:

Fred Bigjim: "Spirit Moves," "Bowhead," "Reindeer," "Bering Coast" from *Sinrock*, Press 22, Portland, Oregon. "A Lone White Arctic Owl" in *Wicazo Sa Review*. "Gaslight" in *Alaska Quarterly Review*'s special issue: "Alaska Native Writers, Storytellers and Orators," Volume 4, Numbers 3 & 4.

Charlie Blatchford: "Why?" and "Magnetized" in the Institute of Alaska Native Arts' *Journal of Alaska Native Arts*.

Nora Marks Dauenhauer: "Chilkoot River," "Willie," and "Listening for Native Voices" were published in *The Droning Shaman*, The Black Current Press, Haines, Alaska. "Spring," "A Poem for Jim Nagataak'w," and "Salmon Egg Puller" in *Alaska Quarterly Review*.

Robert H. Davis: "Hands Moving" in *Akwekon*. All other selections published in *SoulCatcher*, Raven's Bones Press, Sitka, Alaska.

Rose Atuk Fosdick: "Chicken Hill," "Cape Nome" and "Nome Seawall" in *Journal of Alaska Native Arts*.

Roy N. Henry: "Brevig Mission" in *Studies in American Indian Literature (SAIL)* "New Native American Writing Issue," 1990.

Edgar Jackson: "The Sinew of our Dreams," "Magic Word," "The Hunter Sees What is There," and "Self-portrait" in *The Light From Another Country*, Greenfield Review Press, Greenfield Center, N.Y. "Three Songs" and "Letter Home" in *The Clouds Threw This Light*, Institute of American Indian Arts, Santa Fe, N.M.

June McGlashan: "Grandmama's Visit" in *Journal of Alaska Native Arts*.

Renee Matthew: "Woodsman / The One Who Wanders" in *Studies in American Indian Literature (SAIL)* "New Native American Writing Issue," 1990.

Agpik-Robert Mulluk, Jr.: "Kobuk Lake Beckons," "Old Village," "The Loneliest Place," and "Body, Mind and Spirit of a Strong Iñupiaq" in *Journal of Alaska Native Arts*.

Jim Schoppert: "Lay the Dark Hills Dreaming" and "The Effect of Alcohol on Indian People" in *The Greenfield Review*.

Glen Simpson: "Traveling in the Land of the Native Art Historians" and "Front Street" in *Alaska Quarterly Review*.

Sherman Sumdum: "Why?" and "Native Corporation" in *Journal of Alaska Native Arts*.

Mary TallMountain: "The Figure in Clay" from *There is no Word for Goodbye*, Blue Cloud Quarterly, Marvin, S.D. "The Light on the Tent Wall," "Brother Wolverine," "Grandmother's Dream," and "The Women in Old Parkas" from *Matrilineal Cycle*, Open Heart Press.

Winton Weyapuk, Jr.: "On Cape Mountain" in *Journal of Alaska Native Arts*.